Sentencecraft

a course in sentence-combining

Frank O'Hare

GINN AND COMPANY

Acknowledgments

Many people have helped me in my work with sentence-combining, but special recognition is due my colleagues at Florida State University: Roy O'Donnell, Kellogg Hunt, John Simmons, James Barnes, Dean Memering, and James McCrimmon; James Squire, Peter Rosenbaum, and Thomas Devine of the NCTE Committee on Research; John Mellon of Boston University, whose pioneering work with transformational sentence-combining encouraged my research efforts; the many teachers who pilot-tested these materials in their classrooms and suggested improvements which have been incorporated in the text; and my wife Moira, who offered consistently sound advice during the writing of this text and the NCTE research report, *Sentence-Combining.*

Grateful acknowledgment is made to Random House, Inc., for permission to use the sentences on pages 4–9 from "The Eighty-Yard Run" by Irwin Shaw from his book *Selected Short Stories,* © 1955, 1961 by Irwin Shaw.

© Copyright, 1975, by Ginn and Company (Xerox Corporation)

All Rights Reserved

Home Office: Lexington, Massachusetts 02173

0-663-24215-0

Contents

Introduction

Read the four passages below. Group them into pairs that are written on similar topics. Then choose from each pair the piece of writing that seems to you the work of the more mature, the more practiced writer. With your classmates discuss the reasons for your choices.

A. He dipped his hands in the bichloride solution. He shook them. The shake was quick. His fingers were down. His fingers were like the fingers of a pianist. The fingers of the pianist were above the keys.

B. A small girl develops from the glare-frosted sheet of walk, walking barefooted, her bare legs striking and recoiling from the hot cement, her feet curling in, only the outer edges touching.

C. He dipped his hands in the bichloride solution and shook them, a quick shake, fingers down, like the fingers of a pianist above the keys.

D. A girl develops from the sheet of walk. The girl is small. The sheet of walk is glare-frosted. She is walking barefooted. Her bare legs strike the hot cement. Her legs recoil from the hot cement. Her feet curl in. Only the outer edges of her feet are touching the hot cement.

A group of high school students was asked to rank the same selections. As a group, they were at least 90 per cent in agreement that B and C ranked above A and D in terms of writing maturity.

Most students felt that sentences B and C communicated smoothly and economically. "They sound like a real writer's sentences—like a pro's," said one student. "They have an easy flow to them," said another. A third thought their strength lay in their compactness: "They don't use any words unnecessarily."

Students recognized that the content of the sentences in each pair is similar. The differences between sentences A and C are differences in writing, not differences in information. One student put it this way, ". . . the same information can sound and look so different—from almost childish to really sophisticated."

Discussing the examples convinced most of the students that sentence-manipulation skills can make a very real difference in a person's writing.

What Can You Accomplish Through This Course?

This book is based on the premise that everyone can learn to write more powerfully and more effectively. Good writing depends not only on having interesting ideas but on being able to put those ideas on paper. What you have to say is, of course, important. But so also is *how* you say it, and that's what this book will concentrate on. It may not transform you into a professional writer, but if you give it a fair trial it will make you a more confident writer and give you alternative ways of expressing your ideas. It will expand the practical options at your command when you are putting your thoughts into writing.

Writing is not only an art; it is also a craft. Words, phrases, and sentences are like clay in the hands of a craftsman—they are pliable and plastic. Learn to shape and reshape them. Never assume that your first attempt at expressing an idea is the best possible way. There is always another way, often one that is more effective.

Although you'll be concentrating on practicing longer sentences than you may be used to writing, that does not mean that all the sentences in a piece of your writing should be long. You will learn not only to add but to delete, to get rid of the superfluous in an effort to achieve economy and clarity. You'll learn to juxtapose long and short sentences to make them both more effective. A writer who uses only long sentences is likely to sound as dull as one who uses only short sentences. In writing as in life, variety is the spice.

1. Combining a Series of Sentences

The sentence-combining exercises in this first section require only simple operations that already are familiar to you. They will demonstrate the kind of manipulating and combining you will perform as you progress through this book toward greater fluency and increasingly mature sentence styles.

Example A shows how a series of "base" sentences can be combined in a single longer sentence.

A. The blunt nose of the Hindenburg rose from the mooring.
The nose hung a moment in the air.
Then it fell suddenly toward the field. **(AND)**

The blunt nose of the Hindenburg rose from the mooring, hung a moment in the air, and then fell suddenly toward the field.

The last sentence has, of course, been formed by combining the first three. Notice that the words *the nose* and *it* have been deleted, and the word *and* has been added before the third base sentence, as the instruction **(AND)** indicated it should be. Commas were added to keep the final sentence from running together.

The same combining procedure has been used in Example B, but new signals have been added. The signal s̶h̶e̶ instructs you to remove the word *she*. The comma signal **(,)** instructs you to put a comma before its base sentence. The signal **(, AND)** may be read as, "When combining, add a comma and the word *and* before this base sentence."

B. Helen raised her pistol.
S̶h̶e̶ took careful aim. **(,)**
S̶h̶e̶ squeezed off five rapid shots to the center of the target. **(, AND)**

Helen raised her pistol, took careful aim, and squeezed off five rapid shots to the center of the target.

1

Problems

I. Combine each of the following sets of base sentences in a single longer sentence. Write your combined version on the lines provided below each set. In some sets the words that must be removed have been crossed out and comma signals have been given; in others you will have to decide what words to omit and where to place commas. Consider the **(AND)** instruction optional. In some places where it appears you may want to do without the word *and*; in some places where the instruction doesn't appear you may want to include *and*. Let your ear be the guide in making these choices.

1. Battaglia glanced at first base.
   ~~He~~ went into his windup. **(,)**
   Then ~~he~~ threw a hanging curve that Ryan knocked out of the stadium. **(, AND)**

   _____

   _____

2. Parker's friends ate his food.
   ~~They~~ sprawled on his sofa. **(,)**
   ~~They~~ pretended to listen to what he said. **(, AND)**

   _____

   _____

3. The fire raced through the abandoned warehouse.
   ~~The fire~~ leveled it in an hour. **(AND)**

   _____

   _____

4. When Nicola didn't show up for their wedding, David
   walked down to the South Street Bridge.
   He climbed onto the railing. **(,)**
   He made the last dive of his career. **(, AND)**

   _____

   _____

   _____

5. Their home-built sloop rode out a hurricane along the
   Atlantic coast.
   It glided through the narrow channel at Rocky Neck.
   Then, with the voyage all but complete, it sank in six
   feet of water.

   _____

   _____

   _____

   _____

6. Fred dashed into the room.
   He lunged at Knuckles.
   He missed.
   He fell in a heap in the corner.

   _____

   _____

   _____

7. They walked on.
   They were looking at the stars.
   They were talking.
   They were ignoring the deserted look the cottages wore.
   They were pretending not to see the cars that passed them.

   _____

   _____

   _____

   _____

II. The sets of base sentences in this exercise were created by breaking up longer sentences from Irwin Shaw's short story "The Eighty-Yard Run." As you did in the first set of problems, combine each set of base sentences to make a single longer sentence. All the necessary signals have been provided to help you with the first six sentences; after that you're on your own.

1. He smiled a little to himself as he ran.
   ~~He was~~ holding the ball lightly in front of him with his two hands. (,)
   His knees ~~were~~ pumping high. (,)
   His hips ~~were~~ twisting in the almost girlish run of a back in a broken field. (,)

   _____

   _____

   _____

   _____

   _____

2. Darling trotted back.

~~He~~ ~~was~~ smiling. **(,)**

~~He~~ ~~was~~ breathing deeply but easily. **(,)**

~~He~~ ~~was~~ feeling wonderful. **(,)**

~~He~~ ~~was~~ not tired, though this was the tail end of practice and he'd run eighty yards. **(,)**

_____

_____

_____

_____

_____

3. Christian Darling, thirty-five years old, sat on the frail spring grass.

~~The~~ ~~grass~~ ~~was~~ greener now than it ever would be again on the practice field. **(,)**

~~He~~ looked thoughtfully up at the stadium. **(,)**

~~The~~ ~~stadium~~ ~~was~~ a deserted ruin in the twilight. **(,)**

_____

_____

_____

_____

_____

_____

4. She made believe she was going to quit work as soon as Darling found a job, even though she was taking over more responsibility day by day at the magazine.
   She was interviewing authors. (,)
   She was picking painters for the illustrations and covers. (,)
   She was getting actresses to pose for pictures. (,)
   She was going out for drinks with the right people. (,)
   She was making a thousand new friends whom she loyally introduced to Darling. (,)

   _____

   _____

   _____

   _____

   _____

5. He drank some whiskey straight.
   He went into the bathroom where his wife was lying deep in her bath. (AND)
   She was singing to herself. (,)
   She was smiling from time to time like a little girl. (AND)
   She was paddling the water gently with her hands. (,)
   She was sending up a slight spicy fragrance from the bath salts she used. (,)

   _____

   _____

   _____

   _____

6. Darling laughed embarrassedly.
   ~~He~~ looked hard at them sitting there. **(,)**
   ~~They were~~ close to each other. **(,)**
   ~~He~~ shrugged. **(,)**
   ~~He~~ turned. **(,)**
   ~~He~~ went toward his hotel. **(AND)**
   The sweat ~~was~~ breaking out on his face. **(,)**
   ~~It was~~ running down into his collar. **(AND)**

   _____

   _____

   _____

   _____

   _____

7. She looked at him seriously for a moment.
   Then she scrambled around, like a little girl.
   She was kneeling on the seat next to him.
   She grabbed him.
   Her hands were along his ears.
   She kissed him as he sprawled, head back, on the seat
      cushion. **(AND)**

   _____

   _____

   _____

   _____

   _____

8. She knew everybody.
   She condescended to no one.
   She devoured books that Darling had never heard of.
   She walked along the streets of the city.
   She was excited.
   She was at home.
   She was soaking in all the million tides of New York
      without fear, with constant wonder.

   _____

   _____

   _____

   _____

   _____

9. He lay there for five minutes.
   He was looking at the ceiling.
   He was thinking of Flaherty.
   Flaherty would be walking down the street.
   Flaherty would be talking in that booming voice, between
      the girls.
   Flaherty would be holding their arms.

   _____

   _____

   _____

   _____

   _____

10. Darling half-closed his eyes.

He almost saw the boy fifteen years ago reach for
   the pass.

He saw the boy slip the halfback.

He saw the boy go skittering lightly down the field. **(AND)**

His knees were high and fast and graceful.

He was smiling to himself because he knew he was going
   to get past the safety man.

_____

_____

_____

_____

_____

_____

Writing Workshop

At regular intervals throughout this book you will put your sentence-combining skills to practical use in a variety of kinds of writing. In each writing workshop there are choices of topics and often choices of form and style as well. None of the topics in any of the writing workshops is intended merely as an assignment to be written once and forgotten. Instead they are meant to be worked and reworked in an effort to improve them as much as possible before they are considered finished. Ideally, each writing workshop should progress through several stages:

Discussion of all the topics.

Choice of a topic.

"Brainstorming" sessions with other students who have chosen the same topic.

A plan for writing.

A first draft.

Student advice and criticism.

A final version.

In this first writing workshop there are three main choices of topic—Moral Dilemma, Stream of Consciousness, and Public Service Message.

1. A Moral Dilemma

In Mark Twain's *Huckleberry Finn* young Huck is faced with an agonizing moral dilemma. Should he obey the law of the land and betray Jim, a runaway slave, or should he follow the dictates of his conscience, break the law, and risk the eternal damnation he's been told will follow? The young boy's defiant decision: "All right, then, I'll *go* to hell."

Agonizing choice is the stuff that TV dramas, movies, short stories, and novels are made of: people faced with tough decisions. Villains are those who violate our sense of right and wrong by choosing what appears to us as wrong. But sometimes it's not easy to know what is right and what is wrong. For example, even those who regard suicide as an immoral act would be unlikely to condemn the badly crippled Captain Oates, who one night crawled from his tent into a howling blizzard in order to give the remaining members of Scott's Antarctic expedition a chance to survive.

Following are five descriptions of people who face moral dilemmas; a piece of writing could be based on any of these five situations or on a similar one of your own. Your writing might take the form either of a short story in which a character is faced with a moral dilemma or of a play or dialogue among the people involved in a moral dilemma. If you choose to write a play or dialogue, you will have to decide whether the decision has already been made or is still to come.

A. A man serving a life sentence for a murder he did not commit finally escapes. He hides out in a mountain cabin. While he is hiding there, a lost eight-year-old boy near death from hunger and exposure takes refuge in the cabin with him. The boy must have hospital treatment, but the escapee knows that if he tries to get the boy back to safety the search parties will capture him and return him to prison. If he leaves the boy and continues his flight, the child will surely die. What should he do?

B. A wealthy young man is dating a girl who lives with her widowed mother. He considers their relationship a casual thing, but she considers it much more. The girl begins having headaches and it is discovered that she has a brain tumor. The operation required to remove it is a dangerous one, and she fears it. One day, in his efforts to reassure her, the young man tells her that she will be all right and that they will marry when she is well. She survives the operation, but it leaves her blind. Should the man keep his promise, even though he does not love her?

C. The sister of a young doctor learns from her brother that he has given false information to the state medical board when applying for a license to practice his medical specialty. He claims that the false information was unimportant and irrelevant, but she, a doctor herself, has reason to believe that her brother is incompetent in the area for which he will be licensed and that he may endanger the lives of his patients. If she reports him to the licensing board, he will be barred from practicing medicine in any form. If she does nothing, people may suffer. What should she do?

D. During World War II a group of Jews in eastern Europe, doomed to a Nazi concentration camp and probable death, attempts to escape to a neutral country. In the group is a mother with a small baby. At a dangerous border crossing the group crouches in the darkness, waiting for a patrol to pass. Hungry and tired, the baby begins to cry. Someone in the group hisses, "Smother that baby or we're all dead!" What should the mother do?

E. In a really tough math course all grades are on a curve; therefore your grade is directly affected by how well or how poorly others do on the final exam. Someone has acquired a copy of the exam and is black-marketing copies. Over half your classmates have been offered a copy and have bought one. If you take the test cold, your chances of getting a decent grade, and the scholarship you're after, are very low. If you report the group to the teacher, they'll know you're the one who turned them in because you're the only one who hesitated to buy. What do you do?

2. Stream of Consciousness

What goes on inside your head? Do you think in nice, neat, orderly sentences, in "good" English, one idea at a time? Many writers have tried to record the "stream" of things going on inside their heads. It is a surprising jumble of words, sentences, parts of sentences, sights, sounds, bodily sensations, memories and inexplicable notions.

For as long as you can keep it up, try to write down every thought that comes into your mind. Although you will be thinking faster than you can write, try to record as much as you possibly can. Don't concern yourself with spelling and punctuation; you can correct and reorganize later as still other thoughts come to you.

3. Public Service Message

Suppose you were given one page of advertising space in a popular magazine or one minute of time on a television network to use for an appeal to readers to support some cause. It might be an appeal for contributions to the Heart, Cancer, or Muscular Dystrophy foundation; to new voters to get out and vote, no matter what their political affiliation may be; for contributions to fund relief agencies, foreign or domestic, like "CARE," "HOPE," or "Save the Children"; to "Ban the Bomb" or outlaw war, or any other appeal you think worthy.

Compose your message, taking care to consider its visual as well as emotional and rational appeal.

2. Additions to Sentences: when, where, how

Often a sentence indicates not only that a particular event occurred but also when, or where, or how it occurred. This extra information can be provided by adding a "when," "where," or "how" phrase to the sentence. For example:

Ramirez outlined his strategy.

WHEN Ramirez outlined his strategy *before the match.*

WHERE Ramirez outlined his strategy *in the locker room.*

HOW Ramirez outlined his strategy *carefully.*

"Where" phrases quite often begin with words like *at, in, on, by,* or *near;* "when" phrases often begin with words like *before, during, after, at,* or *in;* and "how" phrases often consist of a single word that ends with *ly.*

More than one phrase may be added to a sentence, and the phrases may be added in various positions. The information in the three example sentences given above could all be combined in one sentence:

Ramirez carefully outlined his strategy in the locker room before the match.

Or it could be combined in a different way:

In the locker room before the match Ramirez outlined his strategy carefully.

In this section you will combine groups of sentences so that all the information, including the where, when, and how phrases, is included in a single sentence, as in the following example.

Some men were shouting slogans wildly.
Some men were shouting slogans in the square.

Some men were wildly shouting slogans in the square.
OR
In the square some men were shouting slogans wildly.

Other versions might also be written.

Problems

Write at least two different sentences from the information included in each group. Include *all* the information in *each* sentence you write.

1. Anthony skipped school during the World Series.
   Anthony skipped school every day.
   Anthony skipped school for a week.

   _____

   _____

   _____

2. My car broke down during the winter.
   My car broke down every Monday morning.
   My car broke down at five o'clock.

   _____

   _____

   _____

   _____

3. The soldiers marched in the terrible heat.
   The soldiers marched all day.
   The soldiers marched slowly.
   The soldiers marched through the forest.

   _____

   _____

   _____

4. Jack ran every day.
   Jack ran through the park.
   Jack ran in the morning.
   Jack ran during the summer.
   Jack ran two miles.

   _____

   _____

   _____

5. His captors tortured Colotti at different times.
   His captors tortured Colotti during the day.
   His captors tortured Colotti mercilessly.
   His captors tortured Colotti during the night.
   His captors tortured Colotti for three whole months.

   _____

   _____

   _____

3. Challenge

In this section you will make use of the combining techniques introduced so far.

Problems

I. Combine each of the following sets of base sentences in a single sentence. Comma signals and **(AND)** signals have been given for some sentences.

1. Mark dashed into the street.
   He tripped up the fleeing robber.
   He grabbed the purse.
   He ran for his life.

   _____

   _____

2. The sun beat down on Puerto Vallarta.
   It was drying the streets. **(,)**
   It was coloring the whitewashed houses. **(,)**
   It was rousing Emilia from a deep and dreamless sleep. **(, AND)**

   _____

   _____

3. He set the box carefully on the table.
   He flipped it open. **(,)**
   He froze. **(, AND)**
   He was staring at the stacks of bills. **(,)**

   _____

   _____

4. Clemente dived to the side.
   He caught the ball.
   He rifled it to first.
   He did this all in one motion.

   _____

   _____

   _____

5. The hunter scrambled onto the rock.
   He gently eased up his rifle.
   He methodically adjusted the sights.
   Then he squeezed off a perfect shot.

   _____

   _____

   _____

II. For each set of base sentences write three different single sentences, each containing all the information in the base sentences.

1. My neighbor's dog howls during the full moon.
   My neighbor's dog howls throughout the night.
   My neighbor's dog howls pitifully.

   _____

   _____

   _____

   _____

2. We won last year.
   We won thanks to our determination and teamwork.
   We won regularly.

_____

_____

_____

_____

_____

3. An ancient rooster crows the sun up every day.
   An ancient rooster crows the sun up enthusiastically.
   An ancient rooster crows the sun up at the crack of dawn.
   An ancient rooster crows the sun up on my uncle's farm in
      Ohio.

_____

_____

_____

_____

_____

_____

_____

Writing Workshop

1. A Publicity Campaign

Somewhere near you there may be a problem that affects the daily lives of many people. Often the first step toward solving a social problem is to make people aware that the problem exists. A logical step is to enlist the aid of people in working toward a solution. Choose a local problem of interest to you and design a publicity campaign to make the problem known or to persuade people to work toward its solution or both. Your campaign might draw attention to substandard housing or a local pollution problem. It might advocate changes in school regulations or urge support for a fund-raising agency. It might spotlight the needs of old people in your community, support the creation of a recreation center or playground, or dramatize the need for highway safety.

It could make use of many forms of communication, including posters, speeches, recorded radio or television messages, a "talk show" presentation, handbills, press releases, photographs, and letters to the editor of a local newspaper. Depending on whether you choose merely to expose a problem or to enlist people to solve it, your goal will be to inform or to persuade.

2. Survival

Clip any photograph of a person from a newspaper or magazine. Suppose that, as part of a survival training course, you and this person were paired together to hike 100 miles through rugged wilderness terrain, living off the land. Write an account of the two or three days that you spent together.

3. Scripting a Film or Filmstrip

Find an interesting filmstrip or film and write a script for a spoken soundtrack to accompany it. You may create a simple narration or explanation to suit the film or you may choose to take an ironic or humorous tone. As an alternative, you might create the script for an entirely original film.

Actual film scripts are prepared in two columns. The left-hand column indicates the sound, both background sound and dialogue, to accompany each camera shot. The right-hand column lists each camera shot and describes what the camera will photograph.

19

4. (the fact that), (that), and (join)

The following examples illustrate three sentence-combining procedures. Each of them is much like the other two.

A. Edna was amazed at SOMETHING.
   Ron had forgotten the combination. **(THE FACT THAT)**

   Edna was amazed at the fact that Ron had forgotten the combination.

B. Julio should admit SOMETHING.
   He was there. **(THAT)**

   Julio should admit that he was there.

C. Rose told me SOMETHING.
   She was leaving on the first plane for Tucson. **(JOIN)**

   Rose told me she was leaving on the first plane for Tucson.

In all three examples the second sentence has been added to the first in place of the word SOMETHING. In Example A the sentences are joined by **(THE FACT THAT)**; in Example B they are joined by **(THAT)**; and in Example C they are simply joined without any additional words. Think of the signal SOMETHING as meaning "Put something else in this position." Notice that **(THAT)** and **(THE FACT THAT)** are added to the front of their base sentences before combining.

Problems

Combine each of the following sets of sentences according to the instructions given in parentheses. When more than two sentences are to be combined, combine them step-by-step in the order in which the sentences and instructions are given.

20

1. Tom should have known SOMETHING.
   We'd be leaving early. **(THAT)**

   _____

2. SOMETHING should be proof of my existence.
   I am talking to you. **(THE FACT THAT)**

   _____

   _____

3. Something tells me SOMETHING.
   Fernando's already finished. **(JOIN)**

   _____

   _____

4. Don't let SOMETHING discourage you.
   Your opponent weighs 245 pounds. **(THE FACT THAT)**

   _____

   _____

5. Although they lost their first three meets, Coach Gallagher
   thought SOMETHING.
   Her track team would qualify for the finals. **(JOIN)**

   _____

   _____

   _____

6. Despite all the reports he's heard, The Strangler believes SOMETHING.
   He can defeat The Human Gorilla. **(THAT)**

   _____

   _____

   _____

7. SOMETHING makes me question his alibi.
   There was red clay on Hurley's shoes. **(THE FACT THAT)**

   _____

   _____

8. Claire thought SOMETHING.
   She would never see Frank Robillard again. **(THAT)**

   _____

   _____

9. SOMETHING doesn't necessarily mean SOMETHING.
   I haven't called you. **(THE FACT THAT)**
   I've been too busy. **(THAT)**

   _____

   _____

   _____

   _____

10. In his last message, the trawler's captain said SOMETHING.
    He didn't think SOMETHING. **(THAT)**
    There were icebergs in his area. **(JOIN)**

    _____

    _____

    _____

11. When did you discover SOMETHING?
    Everyone had left. **(THAT)**

    _____

    _____

12. SOMETHING made me fear SOMETHING.
    The birds suddenly stopped singing. **(THE FACT THAT)**
    The storm was about to strike. **(THAT)**

    _____

    _____

    _____

5. (it...that)

Combining with (**IT** . . . **THAT**) is a technique similar to those introduced in Section 4, as the following example illustrates.

> SOMETHING is true.
>
> The world is nearly round. (**IT** . . . **THAT**)
>
> It is true that the world is nearly round.

In the combined sentence the word *it* has replaced SOMETHING and the second sentence has been joined to the first by the word *that*.

Problems

Combine each of the following sets of sentences according to the instructions in parentheses.

1. SOMETHING was obvious to everyone in the courtroom.
   The defendant was covering up for someone in authority.
   (**IT** . . . **THAT**)

   _____

   _____

2. The sweltering tourists couldn't believe SOMETHING.
   Their guide had forgotten the way to the Parthenon. (**THAT**)

   _____

   _____

   _____

   _____

24

3. And SOMETHING came to pass.
   Moses led his people out of the land of Egypt. (IT . . . THAT)

   _____

   _____

4. SOMETHING caused the price of gold to rise sharply.
   Europeans began to lose confidence in the dollar. (THE FACT THAT)

   _____

   _____

5. SOMETHING seems obvious.
   Jim never suspected SOMETHING. (IT . . . THAT)
   He was betrayed by his own family. (THAT)

   _____

   _____

   _____

6. Despite your faith in the wonders of subterranean seepage,
      I think SOMETHING.
   The flowers should be watered. (JOIN)

   _____

   _____

   _____

   _____

7. At a meeting in the mayor's office SOMETHING was
   suggested.
   The contractor should leave all the trees standing. (IT . . . THAT)

   _____

   _____

8. Lynn Melanson has decided SOMETHING.
   A woman's reach should exceed her grasp. (THAT)

   _____

   _____

9. Jerry thought SOMETHING strange.
   None of the Haleys ever went outdoors. (IT . . . THAT)

   _____

   _____

10. SOMETHING should make a strike unnecessary.
    Both labor and management are calling for collective bar-
    gaining. (THE FACT THAT)

   _____

   _____

6. Challenge

In this section you will combine sets of two or more sentences, making use of all the combining techniques introduced in the first seven sections. When combining several sentences, simply follow the combining instructions step-by-step in the order in which they are given. The following example shows the steps in a multiple combining problem as they would appear if someone wrote the results after each step.

SOMETHING makes me think SOMETHING.

We haven't heard from Roger in five days. (THE FACT THAT)

There's trouble ahead. (THAT)

Step 1: The fact that we haven't heard from Roger in five days
         makes me think SOMETHING.

     There's trouble ahead. (THAT)

Step 2: The fact that we haven't heard from Roger in five days
         makes me think that there's trouble ahead.

You may find that working some of the steps out on a piece of scratch paper helps with some of the combining problems. From this section on, the instruction (JOIN) will rarely be used. When the instruction (THAT) appears you should consider it optional; the word *that* may be omitted if the combined sentence seems smoother without it.

Problems

Combine the following sets of sentences according to the instructions.

1. SOMETHING means SOMETHING.
    Jean forgot to pay the electric bill. (THE FACT THAT)
    We'll spend the evening in the dark. (THAT)

    _____

    _____

27

2. I'm sure (of) SOMETHING.
   Raoul told me SOMETHING. (THAT)
   The concert hall had been booked last week. (THAT)

   _____

   _____

3. SOMETHING seems clear.
   Dr. Watson can show the committee SOMETHING. (IT . . . THAT)
   His research offers the best chance of finding a cure. (THAT)

   _____

   _____

4. SOMETHING prevented a panic.
   No one told the audience SOMETHING. (THE FACT THAT)
   A boa constrictor was loose in the stands. (THAT)

   _____

   _____

5. SOMETHING is rumored.
   Senator Keyes will announce SOMETHING. (IT . . . THAT)
   The Defense Department has awarded the contract to a local
      firm. (THAT)

   _____

   _____

   _____

6. SOMETHING ought to indicate SOMETHING.
   Lola spent so much time and did so much research. (THE FACT THAT)
   She was dedicated to the project. (THAT)

   _____

   _____

   _____

7. What famous physicist proved SOMETHING?
   SOMETHING is not true. (THAT)
   A ton of lead is heavier than a ton of feathers. (IT . . . THAT)

   _____

   _____

8. SOMETHING does not necessarily mean SOMETHING.
   Dinosaurs are now extinct. (THE FACT THAT)
   Similar creatures could not roam the earth again. (THAT)

   _____

   _____

   _____

9. SOMETHING was demonstrated by his poor performance in
   the early matches.
   Nolan needs more practice. (THE FACT THAT)

   _____

   _____

10. In a televised address the president declared SOMETHING, SOMETHING, and SOMETHING.

The inflationary spiral must be halted. **(THAT)**

The rate of unemployment should be reduced to less than four per cent. **(THAT)**

SOMETHING was imperative. **(THAT)**

The machinery for implementing these proposals (must) be in operation within 60 days. **(IT . . . THAT)**

_____

_____

_____

_____

_____

Writing Workshop

1. Free Advice

A feature of most newspapers is a column in which people share problems and give advice. Collect several samples of such columns and then either choose one of the following ideas for writing or create an idea of your own based on the advice column.

- Write answers for four of the letters you have found.
- Write a letter of your own detailing a genuine problem. Answer the letter.
- Write a letter describing a fictitious problem. Answer the letter.
- Swap a letter you've written for one written by a classmate. Answer each other's letters.

2. Lies, Whoppers, and Tall Tales

Humor is a uniquely human attribute, and exaggeration is a favorite form of humor. Appoint yourself a member of the Liars Club of America and devote yourself to the creation of a preposterous tall story written in the guise of a true account.

3. The Stars Guide

You are a news reporter for a small weekly newspaper. The person who writes the horoscope column has been confined to a hospital and cannot write his copy for the week. The editor has given you 24 hours to write predictions for the week. If you wish, design a format for your column.

7. (who), (what), (where), (when), (why), and (how)

The six new combining signals in this section operate in similar ways, as the following examples demonstrate.

A. Everyone wondered SOMETHING.

   The heroine's wig kept falling off for some reason. **(WHY)**

   Everyone wondered why the heroine's wig kept falling off.

B. The counter-espionage agents were worried about SOMETHING.

   The odd message might mean something. **(WHAT)**

   The counter-espionage agents were worried about what the odd message might mean.

C. The Langes never knew SOMETHING.

   Someone had left the package outside their door. **(WHO)**

   The Langes never knew who had left the package outside their door.

D. I wonder SOMETHING.

   I left my glasses somewhere. **(WHERE)**

   I wonder where I left my glasses.

E. Do you know SOMETHING?

   The first show starts sometime. **(WHEN)**

   Do you know when the first show starts?

F. I don't understand SOMETHING.

   A radio telescope works somehow. **(HOW)**

   I don't understand how a radio telescope works.

32

In the examples you have just examined, each of the instructions in parentheses directed you to eliminate its corresponding "some" word or phrase, place the instruction word at the beginning of its base sentence, and then insert the result in place of SOMETHING.

Problems

Combine each of the following sets of sentences according to the instructions in parentheses.

1. The engineers soon discovered SOMETHING.
   The drawbridge would not lift for some reason. **(WHY)**

   _____

   _____

   _____

2. The millionaire never understood SOMETHING.
   Something made him so popular. **(WHAT)**

   _____

   _____

   _____

3. Dr. Bergman refused to predict SOMETHING.
   Men would walk on Mars sometime. **(WHEN)**

   _____

   _____

   _____

4. Because he's usually fearless, we couldn't understand
   SOMETHING.
   Hank refused to go skiing for some reason. **(WHY)**

   _____

   _____

5. Eve tried to decide SOMETHING.
   Something made the apple so tempting. **(WHAT)**

   _____

6. Sam tried to discover SOMETHING.
   Spaghetti was grown somewhere. **(WHERE)**

   _____

7. Looking very sheepish, the quarterback tried to explain
   SOMETHING.
   He had run the wrong way somehow. **(HOW)**

   _____

   _____

8. Everybody is wondering SOMETHING.
   Someone painted a frowning face on the Goodenough Tire
   Company's tallest smoke stack. **(WHO)**

   _____

   _____

9. Will someone please tell me SOMETHING?
   All my socks have been hidden somewhere. (WHERE)

   _____

   _____

   _____

10. The weather service couldn't predict SOMETHING.
    The tornado would arrive in our area sometime. (WHEN)

    _____

    _____

    _____

11. Pollsters had a hard time predicting SOMETHING.
    Someone would win the election. (WHO)

    _____

    _____

12. I wish you'd tell me SOMETHING.
    You plan to travel all summer without money somehow. (HOW)

    _____

    _____

    _____

8. (it...) and (how...)

The combining procedures introduced in this section are quite similar to those introduced earlier. Examples A and B illustrate combining processes signaled by **(HOW MUCH)** and **(HOW FAR)**. They resemble the procedures used in Section 7.

A. Norm tried to calculate SOMETHING.

   His money would buy so much food. **(HOW MUCH)**

   Norm tried to calculate how much food his money would buy.

B. Norm tried to calculate SOMETHING.

   He'd have to walk so far. **(HOW FAR)**

   Norm tried to calculate how far he'd have to walk.

   In Examples A and B *how much food* replaced *so much food* and *how far* replaced *so far.* After these "how" phrases were moved to the front of their base sentences, the results were inserted in place of SOMETHING in the first sentence.
   Many **(HOW . . .)** forms are possible. Sentences might be combined using **(HOW LONG), (HOW SERIOUS), (HOW QUIET),** and so on. In each case the combining is accomplished in much the same way.
   The combining in Examples C and D resembles the **(IT . . . THAT)** procedure.

C. SOMETHING doesn't matter to me.

   You go somewhere. **(IT . . . WHERE)**

   It doesn't matter to me where you go.

D. SOMETHING doesn't matter to me.

   You do something. **(IT . . . WHAT)**

   It doesn't matter to me what you do.

(IT . . .) may appear in the six forms **(IT . . . WHO), (IT . . . WHAT), (IT . . . WHERE), (IT . . . WHEN), (IT . . . HOW),** or **(IT . . . WHY).**

Problems

Combine each of the following sets of sentences according to the instructions in parentheses.

1. The police haven't yet estimated SOMETHING.
   The rioters caused so much damage. **(HOW MUCH)**

   _____

2. In his work Pablo Picasso expanded our concept of
   SOMETHING.
   An individual can accomplish so much late in life. **(HOW MUCH)**

   _____

   _____

3. In all these years SOMETHING has never been made clear.
   Someone sent the anonymous donation. **(IT . . . WHO)**

   _____

   _____

4. Nolan knows SOMETHING.
   The movie lasts so long. **(HOW LONG)**

   _____

5. SOMETHING simply can't be determined.
   The problem is so serious. **(IT . . . HOW SERIOUS)**

   _____

6. Dee wanted to know SOMETHING.
   She would need so much material for the costume. **(HOW MUCH)**

   _____

   _____

7. SOMETHING has never seemed more obvious.
   Tax reform is needed so badly. **(IT . . . HOW BADLY)**

   _____

8. SOMETHING isn't really important.
   We'll know the answer so soon. **(IT . . . HOW SOON)**

   _____

9. The newsmen could only guess SOMETHING.
   SOMETHING was not clear for some reason. **(WHY)**
   Ambassador Petronis meant something by his allegations.
      (IT . . . WHAT)

   _____

   _____

10. Mrs. Haley told Mary SOMETHING.
    She would know SOMETHING sometime. **(WHEN)**
    Her experiment would be so reliable. **(HOW RELIABLE)**

    _____

    _____

9. (...to)

Combinations with (. . . TO) are another variation of the combining techniques with (WHO), (WHAT), and the others introduced in Section 7. By comparing the following pairs of examples you will see both the similarities and differences.

A. Collins didn't know SOMETHING.

He was to change gears sometime. (WHEN)

Collins didn't know when he was to change gears.

Collins didn't know SOMETHING.

He was to change gears sometime. (WHEN TO)

Collins didn't know when to change gears.

B. Deciding SOMETHING can be a headache.

One is to buy something for a friend's birthday. (WHAT)

Deciding what one is to buy for a friend's birthday can be a headache.

Deciding SOMETHING can be a headache.

One is to buy something for a friend's birthday. (WHAT TO)

Deciding what to buy for a friend's birthday can be a headache.

Problems

Combine each of the following sets of sentences according to the instructions in parentheses.

1. Mr. Armstrong did not say SOMETHING.

One is to contact someone if a problem should arise. (WHO TO)

---

2. The revolutionary leaders met to decide SOMETHING.
   They were to concentrate their forces somewhere. **(WHERE TO)**

   _____

   _____

3. Although he always faints at the sight of blood, Rupert
   taught a course on SOMETHING.
   One is to handle home injuries somehow. **(HOW TO)**

   _____

   _____

4. Harriet, who was in her first footrace, didn't know
   SOMETHING.
   She was to wait so long for the others to tire. **(HOW LONG TO)**

   _____

   _____

5. The young intern could not decide SOMETHING.
   One is to put so many stitches in the wound. **(HOW MANY TO)**

   _____

   _____

6. The doctor very carefully told his patient SOMETHING.
   His patient was to take the medicine sometime. **(WHEN TO)**

   _____

7. Mrs. Santier hasn't decided SOMETHING.
She should begin teaching Marie SOMETHING sometime. **(WHEN)**
Marie is to drive the family car somehow. **(HOW TO)**

_____

_____

_____

8. Joe hypothesized SOMETHING.
Some birds do not migrate because they cannot decide
   SOMETHING. **(THAT)**
They are to go somewhere. **(WHERE TO)**

_____

_____

9. Hank's field notes have some good information about
   SOMETHING.
One is to find those rare and delicious mushrooms some-
   where. **(WHERE TO)**

_____

_____

10. It will be difficult to decide SOMETHING.
One is to credit someone for that spectacular performance.
   (WHOM TO)

_____

_____

10. Challenge

Problems

Combine each of the following sets of sentences according to the instructions in parentheses.

1. Ryan was surprised to learn SOMETHING.
   No one understood SOMETHING. **(THAT)**
   His paintings represented something. **(WHAT)**

   _____

   _____

2. The philosopher strove all his life to teach humankind SOMETHING.
   Humankind was to tell SOMETHING somehow. **(HOW TO)**
   Something is of value in life. **(WHAT)**

   _____

   _____

   _____

3. SOMETHING is a source of great sadness to Mr. Slekis.
   We still do not know SOMETHING. **(IT . . . THAT)**
   We are to find inner serenity somehow. **(HOW TO)**

   _____

   _____

4. Ms. Hill told Mary Lou SOMETHING.
   Only she could decide SOMETHING. **(THAT)**
   She was to divulge something concerning the conversation
     she had overheard. **(WHAT TO)**

   _____

   _____

5. At first SOMETHING wasn't too clear.
   Manuel had claimed SOMETHING for some reason. **(IT . . . WHY)**
   Funeral directors know SOMETHING. **(THAT)**
   They are to solve grave problems somehow. **(HOW TO)**

   _____

   _____

6. SOMETHING explains SOMETHING.
   The weather has been so unpredictable lately. **(THE FACT THAT)**
   Dee hasn't decided SOMETHING for some reason. **(WHY)**
   She is to begin her 100-mile walk sometime. **(WHEN TO)**

   _____

   _____

7. Do you really believe SOMETHING?
   SOMETHING is determined by SOMETHING. **(THAT)**
   You do so well in life. **(HOW WELL)**
   You are willing to struggle so hard. **(HOW HARD)**

   _____

   _____

8. SOMETHING hasn't been decided.
   One is to sink the piles for the new Morgan Building so deep.
   (IT . . . HOW DEEP TO)

   _____

   _____

9. I was amazed to learn SOMETHING.
   There are so many rooms in the old Scott mansion out on
   River Street. **(HOW MANY)**

   _____

   _____

10. The contestants know only SOMETHING.
    They will be asked SOMETHING. **(THAT)**
    They are someone. **(WHO)**
    They live somewhere. **(, WHERE)**
    They were born sometime. **(, WHEN)**
    They've entered for some reason. **(, AND WHY)**

    _____

    _____

    _____

    _____

Writing Workshop

1. An Advertisement

Create a single ad or an entire advertising campaign for some product, real or imaginary. Begin by collecting examples of ads that you find particularly appealing or particularly offensive. Try to include examples from newspapers, magazines, billboards, radio, and television.

Your own ad might take any of the following forms:

- a newspaper display
- a magazine page
- a billboard
- a radio "spot"
- a television commercial
- a classified ad for publication in the "For Sale," "Swap," or "Trade" column of a local newspaper. You might try to dispose of something you no longer use.

2. An Interview

Write or record an interview with someone, using one of the following suggestions or following a format of your own.

- an interview with a local celebrity, perhaps the oldest resident of the neighborhood
- an imaginary interview with some nationally prominent figure
- man-in-the-street interviews based on a questionnaire
- an imaginary interview between a voluntary "hot line" operator and a caller with a problem
- an interview with a friend concerning some issue on which you differ

For examples of interviews you might turn to radio and television news programs or talk shows, or you might look through newspapers and magazines.

3. Something Makes Me Mad (or Glad)

Suppose that you had a short weekly column in a local newspaper. Devote this week's column to whatever in the world annoys you. Or, if you prefer, write about whatever makes you glad to be alive.

As an alternative, prepare a multi-media presentation based on whatever makes you mad or glad. Make use of whatever facilities you have at your disposal, perhaps including voice, duplicated handouts, posters, displays, slides, tapes, and opaque or overhead projectors.

11. ('s), (ing), (N͟g), and (of)

The four instructions introduced in this section work in combination with each other. The following examples and explanations show how they operate.

A. SOMETHING amazed Coach Jordan.

Leroy ran. (**'s + ING**)

Leroy's running amazed Coach Jordan.

Notice that the instructions apply to the second sentence in the order in which they're given, producing *Leroy's running,* which then replaces SOMETHING in the first sentence.

B. SOMETHING soothed my nerves.

Innumerable bees murmured. (**ING + OF**)

The murmuring of innumerable bees soothed my nerves.

The instructions are applied to the second sentence to produce *The murmuring of innumerable bees,* which replaces SOMETHING in the first sentence.

C. The audience was delighted by SOMETHING.

The girl sang the melody. (**'s + ING + OF**)

The audience was delighted by the girl's singing of the melody.

The girl's singing of the melody results from applying the instructions to the second sentence and replaces SOMETHING in the first.

D. SOMETHING lulled me to sleep.

The sea drones endlessly. (**N͟g + ING + OF**)

The endless droning of the sea lulled me to sleep.

The instruction ~~ly~~ directed you to delete the *ly* from the word *endlessly*. In the combined sentence the changed words appear in the same order as the instructions that changed them.

E. SOMETHING was predictable.

Fisher crushed his opponent ruthlessly. (**'s** + ~~ly~~ + **ING** + **OF**)

Fisher's ruthless crushing of his opponent was predictable.

Again, notice that the changed words in the combined sentence appear in the order in which the instructions were given.

When the (**'s**) instruction is applied, the following changes result:

I becomes *my*

you becomes *your*

he becomes *his*

she becomes *her*

we becomes *our*

they becomes *their*

Problems

Combine each of the following sets of sentences according to the instructions in parentheses.

1. We enjoyed SOMETHING.

   Kathleen sang. (**'s** + **ING**)

   _____

2. Everyone praised SOMETHING.

   The students acted. (**s'** + **ING**)

   _____

3. SOMETHING startled Tony.
   The shutter banged. (**ING + OF**)

   _____

4. SOMETHING caused all the trouble.
   I misinterpreted his message. (**'s + ING**)

   _____

5. SOMETHING made Angela apprehensive.
   The dog howled mournfully. (**'s + ~~BY~~ + ING**)

   _____

6. SOMETHING kept Hannibal from sleeping.
   The elephants bellowed noisily. (**~~BY~~ + ING + OF**)

   _____

7. I can't ignore SOMETHING.
   Jean did not come to my party. (**'s + ING**)

   _____

8. We'll never understand how they entered the city without
      SOMETHING.
   The sentries recognized them. (**s' + ING**)

   _____

   _____

9. Economists have discovered SOMETHING.
   SOMETHING starts a cycle of increases (THAT)
   One country raises its import taxes. ('S + ING)

   _____

   _____

10. SOMETHING delighted Ms. Olivier, who was loaded down with
    mediocre talent.
    Wendy was an accomplished actress. ('S + ING)

    _____

    _____

11. The coach insisted SOMETHING.
    SOMETHING was responsible for SOMETHING. (THAT)
    Lefty pitched accurately. ('S + L̶Y̶ + ING)
    They won the pennant. (S' + ING)

    _____

    _____

    _____

12. Discover → discovery

Many words change their form to indicate a change in their function in a sentence. The basic meaning of the word remains the same despite the change in form. You can say that people *discovered* gold in Alaska or you can talk about their *discovery* of gold. The combining procedure that uses this change in form operates much like the (ING) instruction, as Examples A and B illustrate.

A. We are here to protest SOMETHING.

  The government failed to stop inflation. ('S + FAILURE)

  We are here to protest the government's failure to stop inflation.

B. I could not follow SOMETHING.

  Garcia discussed ribonucleic acids brilliantly.
      ('S + ~~LY~~ + DISCUSSION + OF)

  I could not follow Garcia's brilliant discussion of ribonucleic acids.

Problems

Combine each of the following sets of sentences according to the instructions in parentheses.

1. During the seminar SOMETHING earned a round of applause.

  Tina lucidly described Keynesian economics.
      ('S + ~~LY~~ + DESCRIPTION + OF)

  _____

  _____

  _____

2. SOMETHING brought him national prominence.
   Professor Kwan published his experimental findings.
   ('S + PUBLICATION + OF)

   _____

   _____

3. SOMETHING came as a shock to the National Pickle
   Association.
   The government canceled the cucumber festival.
   ('S + CANCELLATION + OF)

   _____

   _____

   _____

4. SOMETHING is limited to less than 1%.
   This garment shrinks. **(SHRINKAGE + OF)**

   _____

5. SOMETHING brought about SOMETHING.
   Hopkins mismanaged the campaign. **('S + MISMANAGEMENT + OF)**
   Senator Carlotti was defeated in his reelection bid. **('S + DEFEAT)**

   _____

   _____

   _____

   _____

6. When you run into trouble, move for SOMETHING.
   The meeting adjourns. **(ADJOURNMENT + OF)**

   _____

   _____

7. SOMETHING caused observers to question SOMETHING.
   He firmly denied any interest in the award. **('S + ~~IX~~ + DENIAL + OF)**
   He was sincere. **('S + SINCERITY)**

   _____

   _____

   _____

8. SOMETHING confirmed SOMETHING.
   Colonel Singer disappeared mysteriously. **('S + ~~IX~~ + DISAPPEARANCE)**
   I distrusted the security arrangements. **('S + DISTRUST + OF)**

   _____

   _____

   _____

13. (for...to) and (it...for...to)

The following examples illustrate the functions of the **(FOR ... TO)** and **(IT ... FOR ... TO)** instructions.

A. Now is the time (for) SOMETHING.
   All good people come to the aid of their country. **(FOR ... TO)**

   Now is the time for all good people to come to the aid of their country.

B. SOMETHING was easy.
   Maria learned French. **(IT ... FOR ... TO)**

   It was easy for Maria to learn French.

Problems

Combine each of the following sets of sentences according to the instructions in parentheses.

1. The revolving blue light seemed to be a signal (for) SOMETHING.
   We pulled over. **(FOR ... TO)**

   _____

   _____

2. Their allergies made SOMETHING uncomfortable.
   They walked through the fields of flowers. **(IT ... FOR ... TO)**

   _____

   _____

54

3. We're just waiting (for) SOMETHING.
   The captain leads the charge. **(FOR . . . TO)**

   _____

4. SOMETHING was impossible.
   John studied during commercials. **(IT . . . FOR . . . TO)**

   _____

   _____

5. SOMETHING will be a simple matter.
   Dunbarton The Human Fly will lower himself to the jewel
      case. **(IT . . . FOR . . . TO)**

   _____

   _____

6. We've been waiting hours (for) SOMETHING.
   Mrs. Friedenberg returns from the smorgasbord table. **(FOR . . . TO)**

   _____

7. SOMETHING was difficult.
   Mayor Adams listened to SOMETHING. **(IT . . . FOR . . . TO)**
   His own son scathingly indicted SOMETHING.
      ('S + ~~BY~~ + INDICTMENT + OF)
   The city was being run somehow. **(HOW)**

   _____

   _____

8. SOMETHING will take several days.
   We will determine the full extent of the damage. (IT . . . FOR . . . TO)

   _____

   _____

9. The Whitewater Boat Company is looking (for) SOMETHING.
   Someone will race one of their kayaks. (FOR . . . TO)

   _____

   _____

10. SOMETHING won't take long.
    Louella will notice SOMETHING. (IT . . . FOR . . . TO)
    We've left. (THAT)

    _____

    _____

14. Challenge

Problems

Combine each set of sentences according to the instructions given in parentheses.

1. We tried to explain SOMETHING.
   Our English guest could not understand SOMETHING. **(THAT)**
   SOMETHING had caused so much confusion for some reason. **(WHY)**
   He drove on the left-hand side of the road. **('S + ING)**

   _____

   _____

   _____

2. SOMETHING made Anatole wish SOMETHING.
   There was every likelihood of SOMETHING. **(THE FACT THAT)**
   He had to spend the day with his cousin Elmore. **('S + ING)**
   He had stayed home. **(THAT)**

   _____

   _____

   _____

3. The reporter found SOMETHING.
   SOMETHING taught her SOMETHING. **(THAT)**
   She attempted to cover the circus from an unusual angle. **('S + ING)**
   One is to avoid an angry zebra somehow. **(HOW TO)**

   _____

   _____

4. SOMETHING is possible.
   Senator Williams has erred in SOMETHING. (IT . . . THAT)
   He thinks SOMETHING. (ING)
   SOMETHING will not affect SOMETHING. (THAT)
   He votes on the farm subsidy bill somehow. (HOW)
   The rural voters accept him. (S' + ACCEPTANCE + OF)

   _____

   _____

   _____

   _____

5. SOMETHING explains SOMETHING.
   They had found no circular topographical features.
      (THE FACT THAT)
   Early navigators concluded SOMETHING for some reason. (WHY)
   SOMETHING was the result of SOMETHING. (THAT)
   Their sailing ships disappeared mysteriously.
      (THE + ɪ𝐘 + DISAPPEARANCE + OF)
   These vessels had plunged off the edge of the world. (S' + ING)

   _____

   _____

   _____

   _____

   _____

6. SOMETHING was disturbing.
   The guide hinted SOMETHING. (IT . . . FOR . . . TO)
   She was confused about SOMETHING. (THAT)
   We were headed somewhere. (WHERE)

   _____

   _____

7. Because he never pays any attention to SOMETHING, SOMETHING
      will take days.
   The instructions say something. (WHAT)
   Thurston will figure out SOMETHING. (IT . . . FOR . . . TO)
   He is to assemble the miniature helicopter somehow. (HOW TO)

   _____

   _____

   _____

   _____

8. SOMETHING is unlikely.
   SOMETHING will make SOMETHING easier. (IT . . . THAT)
   Margery has tied a string around her finger. ('S + ING)
   She will remember her appointment with the dentist.
      (IT . . . FOR . . . TO)

   _____

   _____

   _____

9. I don't think SOMETHING.
   SOMETHING makes SOMETHING inevitable. **(THAT)**
   Our oil and gas reserves are depleted. **(THE + DEPLETION + OF)**
   Industrial production will simply grind to a halt. **(IT ... THAT)**

   _____

   _____

   _____

10. Panic struck the passengers when the loudspeakers blared
    SOMETHING.
    The captain announced SOMETHING. **('S + ANNOUNCEMENT)**
    An explosion in the engine room made SOMETHING neces-
    sary. **(THAT)**
    Everyone abandons ship. **(IT ... FOR ... TO)**

    _____

    _____

    _____

11. A group of dentists recently announced SOMETHING.
    Extensive research indicated SOMETHING. **(THAT)**
    SOMETHING results in SOMETHING. **(THAT)**
    Sugar is restricted in a person's diet. **(A RESTRICTION + OF)**
    Tooth decay is reduced dramatically. **(⊠ + REDUCTION + OF)**

    _____

    _____

    _____

12. SOMETHING led to SOMETHING.

   Judge Buros discovered serious contradictions in the star
      witness's testimony. (**'S + DISCOVERY + OF**)

   He declared a mistrial. (**'S + ING**)

   _____

   _____

   _____

13. Some of the art experts suggested SOMETHING.

   SOMETHING may have caused SOMETHING. (**THAT**)

   The sculpture was exposed to urban air pollution. (**'S + ING**)

   It deteriorated. (**'S + DETERIORATION**)

   _____

   _____

   _____

Writing Workshop

1. Writing for Two Audiences

Write a letter to two very different people telling them about something you've done or something that has happened to you. You might imagine what could happen on a particularly bad day. Use the same basic facts in both letters, but change the tone and style to suit the different audiences.

As an alternative to writing a letter, you could write out the dialog that an audio tape recorder would pick up if it were recording telephone conversations between you and the two different audiences.

2. A Job Application

A. Imagine you are out of work and have just seen or heard of exactly the job you are looking for. Write a letter applying for that job, giving your would-be employer all the information he'll need in as economical and efficient a way as possible.

If you can't think of a job you might want, clip a help wanted ad from a newspaper and write an application for that job.

Write a second letter of application guaranteed *not* to get you the job.

B. Or imagine that you are the friend of someone who desperately needs a job. Write a letter to an employer to help your friend get the job.

C. Some jobs are never applied for, yet people do get them. Invent suitable applications for such jobs. Here are a few possibilities:

Brain surgeon

President of the USA

International spy

Flag pole sitter

Hole maker in a doughnut factory

Jewel thief

15. Repetition as a Combining Signal, Part I

In previous sentence-combining problems, when SOMETHING has been used as a combining signal it has been replaced by an entire sentence after certain changes have been made. Beginning with this section, you'll be combining some sentences without the aid of the SOMETHING signal. Instead, the signal for combining will be a word or phrase that is repeated. The following examples illustrate the technique.

A. Most of the helicopters were already beyond repair.

   The terrorists destroyed the helicopters. **(THAT)**

   Most of the helicopters that the terrorists destroyed were already beyond repair.

B. We're looking for the person.

   The person installed a microphone in this potted palm. **(WHO)**

   We're looking for the person who installed a microphone in this potted palm.

Notice that the repeated phrase is removed from the second sentence and replaced by the instruction word. The result is inserted in the first sentence just after the word or phrase that was repeated. The instructions **(WHICH)**, **(THAT)**, **(WHO)**, and **(WHOM)** will be used in this section. Sometimes the instruction **(WHICH/THAT)** will be given, indicating that you should choose between the two.

Problems

Combine each of the following sets of sentences according to the instructions given in parentheses. Three sets of sentences have no signals to help you. Decide for yourself how those sentences should be combined.

1. Although it is usually quiet during the week, the amusement park is very busy on weekends.
   The amusement park opened just last year. **(WHICH)**

   _____

   _____

2. A student is liable to go crazy.
   A student spends all year in the library. **(WHO)**

   _____

3. The bandit slipped through the forest.
   The Pinkerton men were tracking the bandit. **(WHOM/JOIN)**

   _____

   _____

4. The heavy clouds ruined what had been a beautiful day.
   The heavy clouds rolled in from the west. **(THAT)**

   _____

   _____

5. I've always wanted to meet someone.
   Someone could explain how a doughnut machine works. **(WHO)**

   _____

   _____

6. Andy returned the skates.
   He had borrowed the skates last year.

   _____

   _____

7. Gayle turned out to be the most reliable member of our
   team.
   We had never trusted Gayle. **(WHOM)**

   _____

   _____

8. Anybody must be either tremendously brave or ridiculously
   foolish.
   Anybody would climb that mountain in this storm.

   _____

   _____

9. That horse has never won a race.
   That horse was sold last year for more than a hundred thousand dollars.

   _____

   _____

16. Repetition as a Combining Signal, Part II

In this section you'll add the instructions **(WHOSE)**, **(WHEN)**, **(WHERE)**, and **(WHY)** to the use of repetition as a combining signal. Notice that the repetition may not always be precisely word-for-word.

Problems

Combine each of the following sets of base sentences according to the instructions given in parentheses. If there are no instructions, decide for yourself how the sentences should be combined.

1. It was an ancient language.
   The ancient language's words were mainly those of wonder and delight. **(WHOSE)**

   _____

   _____

2. After a wild chase through downtown traffic, Mr. Attaya was able to identify the gas station.
   The thieves had hidden the jewels in the gas station. **(WHERE)**

   _____

   _____

3. Inspiration came to her at a time.
   At that time she needed encouragement. **(WHEN)**

   _____

   _____

4. The collie was the animal.
   The collie attracted all the attention. **(THAT)**
   I liked the animal the least. **(THAT)**

   _____

   _____

5. We were looking for that rare person.
   That rare person's sole purpose in life was to make other
   people happy. **(WHOSE)**

   _____

   _____

6. The room was lit by a single spotlight.
   The diamond was displayed in the room. **(WHERE)**
   The spotlight was trained on the gem itself. **(WHICH/THAT)**

   _____

   _____

7. Give me one good reason.
   I shouldn't refuse to help you for that reason.

   _____

8. She longed for a time.
   At that time explanations would no longer be necessary.

   _____

9. The person doesn't deserve much sympathy.
   George was quarreling with the person. **(WHOM)**

   _____

10. Because it involved the national security, he could not tell
    his wife the reason.
    He was friendly with those underworld characters for that
    reason. **(WHY)**

    _____

    _____

17. Challenge

Both SOMETHING and repeated phrases will be used as combining signals in this section.

Problems

Combine each set of sentences according to the instructions in parentheses. When no instructions are given, decide for yourself how the sentences should be combined.

1. The starter told the jockeys SOMETHING.

   The starter was nervously chewing a cigar.

   They were to bring their mounts up to the starting gate sometime.

   _____

   _____

   _____

2. SOMETHING is certainly possible.

   Creatures from the oceans could adapt to a gaseous environment. (IT . . . THAT)

   Scientists have been trying to develop this environment recently. (THAT/WHICH)

   _____

   _____

   _____

3. Juan was interested to learn SOMETHING.
   Books describe SOMETHING. **(THAT)**
   Books were written about this region. **(THAT)**
   Early explorers attempted to find a subterranean city.
   (S' + ATTEMPTS)

   _____

   _____

4. Mr. Dudley considers SOMETHING arrogant.
   Humans assume SOMETHING. **(IT . . . FOR . . . TO)**
   They are the only species. **(THAT)**
   The species will never become extinct. **(THAT)**

   _____

   _____

5. SOMETHING came as no surprise.
   Alice declared SOMETHING sometime. **(IT . . . WHEN)**
   The stronghold is the male-dominated medical profession. **(THAT)**
   Women must attack the stronghold next. **(THAT/JOIN)**

   _____

   _____

6. I get nervous every time Tom goes mountain climbing
   because he is convinced (of) SOMETHING.
   SOMETHING is impossible. **(THAT)**
   He loses his balance. **(IT . . . FOR . . . TO)**

   _____

   _____

7. SOMETHING exasperated Eleanor.
   The customs official meticulously scrutinized her purse.
   ('S + ~~HER~~ + SCRUTINY + OF)
   Eleanor sarcastically asked SOMETHING. (WHO)
   SOMETHING would take so much time. (HOW MUCH)
   He finishes SOMETHING. (IT . . . FOR . . . TO)
   He examines the rest of their luggage. ('S + EXAMINATION + OF)

   _____

   _____

   _____

   _____

8. I think SOMETHING's unfair.
   The committee makes us wait three days for SOMETHING.
      (IT . . . FOR . . . TO)
   They announce SOMETHING. (S' + ANNOUNCEMENT + OF)
   They've chosen someone as chairman. (WHOM/WHO)

   _____

   _____

   _____

9. How can they find anyone?
   Anyone meets all the requirements. (WHO)
   They've specified all the requirements. (THAT/JOIN)

   _____

Writing Workshop

1. A Children's Story

A. Write a story that would be read to first grade children. Illustrate it if you like. Try to include plenty of action and maintain a fast pace. Remember that your audience has watched more than its share of rapid-fire television shows. Consider the vocabulary level of your story carefully. Try reading your story to a first-grade class or to as many six- or seven-year-olds as you can find. You are likely to find them formidable critics. If they enjoy your story, you might think of sending it to a publisher.

B. Re-write a well known children's story or nursery rhyme as a television news item, as a parody, or in a very up-to-date style intended for the child steeped in popular culture.

Feel free to change the story as necessary, but your audience should be able to recognize its source.

2. Television Characters

In play or short story form, write about an episode in the life of a television character or characters your audience already knows. Either invent an entirely new episode or take the character beyond the televised action of an episode you've seen. It might be a comedy, a detective story, a western or a thriller. You might even include commercials. If possible, produce a live or taped performance of your story.

3. Music and Song

A. Pick an interesting tune and write new lyrics for it. Get someone to sing it. Tape the result.

B. Write a parody of a well known song—preferably a romantic one. *Mad* magazine is a source for models of this type of parody. You might add the finishing touch by having the new song sung by someone who can imitate a sincere but untalented singer.

18. Underlining as a Combining Signal, Part I

In most of the combining problems you've worked so far, you've rearranged a base sentence according to an instruction in parentheses, and then inserted the result into another base sentence. In this section you'll be writing combinations without using parenthesized instructions, as the following examples demonstrate.

A. The girl suddenly screamed in terror.
   The girl was feeding Dr. Boulake's experimental animals.

   The girl feeding Dr. Boulake's experimental animals suddenly screamed in terror.

B. The oil paintings are worth millions of dollars.
   The paintings are to be put up for auction tomorrow.

   The oil paintings to be put up for auction tomorrow are worth millions of dollars.

C. The children are innocent victims of the war.
   The children are in this orphanage.

   The children in this orphanage are innocent victims of the war.

D. Blanche easily pulled away from the field.
   Blanche is a powerful runner.

   Blanche, a powerful runner, easily pulled away from the field.

As you can see, the new procedure involves eliminating repeated words and any form of *be* before the result is inserted after the first appearance of the repeated words. In each case the underlining itself is the combining signal, and no parenthesized instruction is necessary. The underlining signal simply instructs you to keep the words that are underlined and eliminate those that are not. Notice that Example D is somewhat different from the others and that commas must be added before and after the inserted phrase.

Problems

Combine each of the following sets of sentences according to the instructions given. When no instructions are given, decide for yourself how the sentences should be combined.

1. The space administration has chosen several people.
   The people are to live in orbiting space stations.

   _____

   _____

2. The articles are missing.
   The articles were to be sold next week.

   _____

   _____

3. The strangers are searching for treasure.
   The strangers are diving in the lagoon.
   The treasure was lost there centuries ago.

   _____

   _____

4. Raoul's ability was shared by Miguel.
   His ability was to predict the future.
   Miguel was his greatest rival.

   _____

   _____

5. The governor stressed SOMETHING.
   She believed SOMETHING. (**'S + BELIEF**)
   Hospitals must be financed through taxes. (**THAT**)
   Hospitals are for the poor and aged.
   The taxes are on luxuries.

   _____

   _____

   _____

6. Mayor Albert declared SOMETHING.
   New taxes cannot be paid by people.
   The taxes are on excess income.
   The people are unemployed.

   _____

   _____

   _____

   _____

7. Adelaide had her studio in a houseboat.
   Adelaide was a brilliant young painter.
   The houseboat was destroyed by the recent hurricane.

   _____

   _____

   _____

8. The pollution control commission was not impressed by SOMETHING.
   Detroit claimed SOMETHING. ('S + CLAIM)
   Most cars have efficient emission control devices. (THAT)
   The cars are <u>being produced today.</u>

   _____

   _____

   _____

9. The kids seemed to get more enjoyment from SOMETHING than from SOMETHING.
   The kids were <u>around us at the rock concert.</u>
   The kids talked about the performers. (ING)
   The kids listened to the music. (ING)

   _____

   _____

   _____

10. Sanborn's last pass was dropped by hands.
    The pass was desperate.
    The hands were too numb to grip the ball.

    _____

    _____

19. Underlining as a Combining Signal, Part II

In all of the combining problems in Section 18 the underlined portion of the second sentence was inserted into the first immediately after the repeated words. Sometimes it is necessary to make the insertion before the first appearance of the repeated words, as in the following example.

Most Latin Americans enjoy soccer.
The Latin Americans are <u>youthful</u>.

Most youthful Latin Americans enjoy soccer.

How can you tell when to insert the underlined word or words before the first appearance of the repeated words? There are two ways. First, the underlined portion is usually just a single word, like *youthful;* a hyphenated word, like *nerve-shattering;* or a single word preceded by a word ending in *-ly,* like *finely chopped.* Second, the combined sentence will not sound right if the insertion is made in the wrong place. Your experience as a speaker and writer of English will tell you where to insert the underlined words. Let your ear be your guide. Surely your ear would reject something like the following:

Latin Americans youthful enjoy soccer.

Problems

Combine each of the following sets of sentences according to the instructions given. When no instructions are given, combine as you think best. Keep the following points in mind as you work the problems with underlining: (1) eliminate the second appearance of the repeated words and any form of *be;* (2) insert the underlined word or words to the left or right of the first appearance of the repeated words, depending on which sounds better; (3) use commas where needed.

1. The sheep stood suddenly.
   The sheep was <u>sleeping</u>.

   _____

2. The Secretary of Defense asserted SOMETHING.
   An offensive capability is a necessity. **(THAT)**
   The offensive capability is <u>powerful</u>.
   The necessity is <u>absolute</u>.

   _____

   _____

3. A team of surgeons worked to save the driver.
   The surgeons were experienced.
   The driver was injured.

   _____

4. Eileen sampled the ants.
   The ants were <u>chocolate-covered</u>.
   She was <u>in a state of nervous confusion</u>.

   _____

5. Haze obscured the sun over Chicago.
   The haze was <u>thick</u> and <u>gray</u>.
   The sun was <u>pale</u>.

   _____

   _____

6. The exiles pleaded with the officials.
   The exiles were dejected.
   The officials were uncompromising.

   _____

7. The heart of the blaze was a mass of light and heat.
   The mass was pulsing.
   The light was ruby.
   The heat was searing.

   _____

   _____

8. Several animals were shot by hunters.
   The animals were <u>considered "rare and endangered species."</u>
   The hunters were <u>careless</u>.

   _____

   _____

9. Congressman Bigelow refused to support budget reductions.
   The budget reductions were <u>stringent</u>.
   <u>But</u> they were <u>equitable</u>.
   They were <u>affecting his constituency</u>.

   _____

   _____

10. Lord Dudley found himself in a pit.
    Lord Dudley was <u>a renowned naturalist</u>.
    The pit was <u>full of mambas</u>.
    The mambas were <u>hissing</u>.
    The mambas were <u>darting</u>.
    The mambas were <u>venomous</u>.
    Mambas are <u>the deadliest of snakes</u>.

    _____

    _____

11. The apprentice glanced nervously at the lion tamer.
    The apprentice was <u>ashen-faced</u>.
    The apprentice was alone in the cage for the first time. **(WHO)**
    The lion tamer nodded reassuringly. **(WHO)**

    _____

    _____

12. Casey stepped before the fans.
    Casey was called Mighty.
    Casey was cool.
    Casey was calm.
    Casey was confident.
    The fans were from Mudville.
    The fans cheered their hero wildly.

    _____

    _____

    _____

20. Challenge

Combine each of the following sets of sentences according to the instructions. When no instructions are given, combine the sentences as you think best.

1. SOMETHING is unlikely.
   A worker can easily be convinced (of) SOMETHING. (IT . . . THAT)
   The worker is a <u>migrant</u>.
   The worker is <u>earning less than a subsistence wage</u>.
   All men are equal under the law. (THAT)

   _____

   _____

   _____

2. The next letter comes from a viewer.
   The viewer doesn't understand SOMETHING. (WHO)
   A polar bear would know SOMETHING somehow. (HOW)
   A polar bear is <u>living in the Arctic region</u>.
   The sun never sets in the Arctic region. (WHERE)
   The bear is to go to sleep sometime. (WHEN TO)

   _____

   _____

   _____

   _____

3. The reporters had been informed (of) SOMETHING.
   They were from Eyeopener News.
   They were probing corruption in sports.
   The challenger would throw the fight in the eighth round.
   The challenger was way ahead on points.

   _____

   _____

   _____

4. Mr. Hamm's concern was SOMETHING.
   He was to locate a hair piece somewhere. **(WHERE TO)**
   The hair piece would be efficient enough to disguise the
     patches.
   The patches were bald.
   The patches threatened his film career. **(WHICH/THAT)**

   _____

   _____

   _____

5. Ambassador Philpot saw SOMETHING.
   The courier was watching his face. **(THAT)**
   The courier was dreadfully anxious to know SOMETHING.
   He thought something about the message. **(WHAT)**

   _____

   _____

   _____

6. Thelma is convinced (of) SOMETHING.
   Thelma has only recently learned SOMETHING. **(WHO)**
   She executes a *pas de deux*. **(HOW TO)**
   She'll never perfect the many routines. **(THAT)**
   The routines are <u>intricate</u>.
   The routines are <u>required of a prima ballerina</u>.

   _____

   _____

   _____

   _____

   _____

7. SOMETHING meant SOMETHING.
   Coach Whittier realized SOMETHING. **('S + REALIZATION)**
   He would have to sign a quarterback. **(THAT)**
   The quarterback is <u>experienced</u>.
   The quarterback is <u>talented enough to lead the team to the
   playoffs</u>.
   He would have to trade one of his star linebackers. **(THAT)**

   _____

   _____

   _____

   _____

   _____

8. Professor Eckerd was convinced (of) SOMETHING.
   She was <u>an oceanographic researcher.</u>
   Engineers could not learn SOMETHING without SOMETHING. **(THAT)**
   The engineers were to construct living quarters somehow.
   (HOW TO)
   The living quarters were <u>efficient.</u>
   The living quarters were <u>underwater.</u>
   Volunteers live in models. **(S' + ING)**
   The models were <u>experimental.</u>
   They were to live there <u>for an extended period of time.</u>

   _____

   _____

   _____

9. The state will make a museum of the fort.
   The fort is old.
   The fort is stone.
   The fort overlooks Lake Jackson.

   _____

   _____

10. Several pieces of sculpture were restored by experts.
    The pieces of sculpture were <u>damaged by soot.</u>
    The soot was <u>from nearby factories.</u>
    The experts were <u>hastily summoned.</u>

    _____

    _____

11. Many people have argued SOMETHING.
    The people are concerned.
    They are looking for a life.
    The life will be better.
    The life will be more meaningful.
    We must recognize SOMETHING.
    We are interdependent.

    _____

    _____

    _____

    _____

12. The people were terrified by SOMETHING.
    The people were in the housing project.
    The project was near the gas storage tanks.
    Something exploded deafeningly. (A + ~~IT~~ + EXPLOSION)
    The explosion rocked their buildings. (WHICH/THAT)
    It smashed dishes. (ING)
    It cracked ceilings. (ING)
    It broke windows. (ING)

    _____

    _____

    _____

    _____

13. The coach threw down his playbook.
    He slumped in his chair for a couple of hours. **(AND)**
    He watched television. **(ING)**
    He thought of the game. **(ING)**
    He was <u>desperate for the victory.</u>
    He knew SOMETHING. **(ING)**
    He'd never get it. **(THAT)**

    _____

    _____

    _____

    _____

14. The man gathered the boy into his arms.
    The man was old.
    The man was grief-stricken.
    The man was certain (of) SOMETHING.
    The boy was dying.
    The man stumbled home.
    He sank to his knees at home.
    He prayed SOMETHING.
    His son would recover.

    _____

    _____

    _____

    _____

    _____

15. The manufacturers didn't think SOMETHING.

The manufacturers had designed the new cafeteria furniture. (WHO)

SOMETHING was fair. (THAT)

The consumer protection agency tested it with a mob of kids. (IT . . . FOR . . . TO)

The kids were <u>unruly</u>.

The kids gouged it with forks and knives. (WHO)

The kids <u>marched along the table tops</u>. (AND)

_____

_____

_____

_____

_____

Writing Workshop

1. Obituary Column

A. A local newspaper has given you space in their obituary column for 500 words memorializing any dead person you wish. Choose someone and write your memorial tribute.

B. Write a mock obituary mourning the death of selflessness, 5¢ candy bars, the internal combustion engine, morality, or something else that you feel has passed away.

2. Ghost–writer

Write a biographical account of some incident from a classmate's life based on an interview or on notes your classmate supplies.

3. Daydreams and Nightmares

A. Plan the perfect day. What would you do? Where would you go? With whom? If you're fortunate enough to have enjoyed such a day, tell about it. How did it feel?

B. What or who would you like to be? A super-hero? A millionaire? A star? A hermit? President? Write a daydream, a story about yourself as you'd like to be.

C. What is the worst thing you've ever imagined happening to you? Describe it in all its ghastly detail.

21. Connecting Words

One of the simplest ways to combine two sentences is to join them with a connecting word that establishes a relationship between them, often a relationship that might be hard to establish by any other means. The following examples illustrate several ways in which this can be done.

A. They were happy.
   Their team had won. **(BECAUSE)**

   They were happy because their team had won.

B. The troops came home.
   The war ended. **(AFTER)**

   The troops came home after the war ended.

C. The war ended. **(AFTER)**
   The troops came home.

   After the war ended, the troops came home.

The relationships indicated by connecting words are usually those of cause-and-effect, time, or similarity and difference. Some connecting words are *as soon as, just when, after, before, although, if,* and *since.* In addition, the connection may sometimes be made with a semicolon **(;)** without any additional words, as Example D shows.

D. The war ended.
   The troops came home. **(;)**

   The war ended; the troops came home.

89

Problems

Combine each of the following sets of sentences according to the instructions given.

1. He reached the top of the stairs. **(WHEN)**
   The entire house started to shake.
   Demons had loosed their wrath on it. **(AS IF)**
   The demons were furious.

   _____

   _____

   _____

   _____

2. I don't get there by midnight. **(IF)**
   Come looking for me.
   I'll be in trouble. **(;)**

   _____

   _____

   _____

3. He always quits.
   You need him. **(JUST WHEN)**

   _____

   _____

4. Night came. **(WHEN)**
   We sat huddled in blankets.
   The blankets were thick and woolly.
   It was time to turn in. **(LONG BEFORE)**

   _____

   _____

5. I'll finish that job.
   The parts are sent in by the supplier. **(AS SOON AS)**

   _____

   _____

6. I agree with your second proposal. **(ALTHOUGH)**
   I cannot accept your first.
   It is based on a logical fallacy. **(BECAUSE)**

   _____

   _____

7. You put it that way. **(SINCE)**
   SOMETHING is impossible.
   I disagree with your proposal. **(IT . . . FOR . . . TO)**

   _____

   _____

   _____

8. The students were asked to pass in their papers.
   The students had not finished when the bell rang. **(WHO)**
   They heard the signal. **(AS SOON AS)**
   Their teacher had promised SOMETHING. **(EVEN THOUGH)**
   They would be permitted to complete their work during the
   break. **(THAT)**

   _____

   _____

   _____

   _____

9. To err is human.
   To forgive is divine. **(;)**

   _____

10. They delivered three barrels of wine and seven wheels of
    cheese.
    The barrels were oaken.
    The wine was red.
    The wheels of cheese were great.
    They forgot the glassware and plates. **(BUT)**

    _____

    _____

    _____

    _____

11. You steal the floor plans. **(AFTER)**
    Wait.
    You receive further instructions from the Clandestine Activ-
       ities Center. **(UNTIL)**

    _____

    _____

    _____

12. You fly off the handle. **(BEFORE)**
    You'd better get all the facts.

    _____

    _____

13. The cyclone struck. **(BEFORE)**
    The air seemed heavy and still.

    _____

    _____

22. (ing) and (with)

Some effective sentences can be constructed by changing a word to its -ing form or by using *with* as a connector. Notice the combining procedures illustrated in the following examples.

A. Joe <u>burst through the line</u>. **(ING)**

    Joe forced the quarterback to eat the ball on the fourth down.

    Bursting through the line, Joe forced the quarterback to eat the ball on the fourth down.

B. The angry crowd <u>fell on the assassin</u>. **(ING)**

    The angry crowd tore him limb from limb.

    Falling on the assassin, the angry crowd tore him limb from limb.

C. She was a sensuous beauty.

    She had long auburn hair. **(WITH)**

    She was a sensuous beauty with long auburn hair.

D. The car was in a four-wheel drift. **(WITH)**

    She counter-steered and went on to take the lead.

    With the car in a four-wheel drift, she counter-steered and went on to take the lead.

Problems

Combine each of the following sets of sentences according to the instructions given.

94

1. It was a wild wet day.
   The wind was slapping at my face. **(WITH)**
   The wind <u>chilled me through and through</u>. **(ING)**

   _____

   _____

   _____

2. Alex was <u>lonely</u>.
   Alex was <u>disillusioned</u>.
   Alex was <u>bitter</u>.
   Alex shuffled into the bus station.
   <u>His shoulders</u> were <u>bowed</u>.
   <u>His suitcase</u> was <u>heavy in his hand</u>.

   _____

   _____

   _____

   _____

3. The children were <u>startled by a sudden noise</u>.
   The children took off down the hill.
   Dracula was after them. **(AS THOUGH)**

   _____

   _____

   _____

4. Robert was <u>dedicated</u>.
   Robert was <u>honest</u>. **(AND)**
   Robert was doomed to failure in a society.
   The society sneered at dedication. **(THAT)**
   The society <u>refused to acknowledge selfless commitment</u>. **(AND)**

   _____

   _____

   _____

5. The deer <u>sensed danger</u>. **(ING)**
   The deer lifted its head.
   Its <u>ears</u> were stiff and <u>straight</u>.
   Its <u>body</u> was <u>tense</u>.
   It was <u>ready to explode into motion at the slightest sound</u>.

   _____

   _____

   _____

6. The monster lurched toward us.
   The monster was <u>foul-smelling</u>.
   The monster was <u>bloated</u>.
   The monster was <u>decayed</u>. **(AND)**
   It had hollow sockets for eyes. **(WITH)**

   _____

   _____

   _____

7. You got beyond those pious utterances about his concern
     for the weak and oppressed. **(WHEN)**
You realized SOMETHING.
He was quite simply an egomaniac. **(THAT)**
He had no other concern but his own ambition. **(WITH)**

_____

_____

_____

8. They were hand in hand.
They walked on in silence.
The wind stirred the moist, warm air. **(ING)**
The tide swept rhythmically over their bare feet. **(ING)**
The sand was cool and liquid on their toes.

_____

_____

_____

9. The kids were bursting with excitement.
The kids all spoke at once.
Each one tried to get my attention. **(ING)**
Each one tried to out-shout the others. **(ING)**
No one made any sense. **(ING)**

_____

_____

_____

10. Madeline dashed into the room. **(ING)**
    Madeline dived at the thief.
    Madeline beat him into submission.
    Madeline tied him up.
    She was about to be kissed by the handsome scientist. **(AND, JUST AS)**
    She had just saved the handsome scientist's life. **(WHOSE)**
    She was awakened by the jingle of her alarm clock.
    The jingle was insipid.
    The jingle was mocking.

    _____

    _____

    _____

    _____

    _____

    _____

11. Julia stood at the edge of the cliff.
    She looked down on their upturned, nickel-sized faces by
       the side of the tidal pool. **(ING)**
    She wished she had ignored the dare. **(ING)**
    She felt trapped. **(ING)**
    Yet she knew SOMETHING. **(ING)**
    She couldn't back down. **(THAT)**

    _____

    _____

    _____

    _____

12. The attendant stumbled out of his shack.
    He was an emaciated looking fellow.
    The fellow had white hair and skin the color of an old saddle. **(WITH)**
    He stood scowling at us. **(AND)**
    His chin was thrust forward. **(WITH)**
    His eyes were blazing.

    _____

    _____

    _____

    _____

23. Colon and Dash

The colon (:) and dash (—) are useful devices favored by many writers. The following examples show the combining that might have led to four sentences taken from the work of professional writers. The colon and dash signals instruct you to put a colon or dash in front of the base sentence.

A. He had managed to buy also a coral necklace for his small daughter.
   It was a coral necklace naturally. (:)
   Her name was Coralie. (SINCE)

   He had managed to buy also a coral necklace for his small daughter: a coral necklace naturally, since her name was Coralie.

   MacKinlay Kantor

B. He pushed back the chair a few feet.
   A full view of himself was available in the tilted mirror. (SO)
   He was a tall, narrow-skulled, smooth-cheeked youth. (:)
   The youth was tightly dressed in darkest gray.

   He pushed back the chair a few feet, so a full view of himself was available in the tilted mirror: a tall, narrow-skulled, smooth-cheeked youth, tightly dressed in darkest gray.

   John Updike

C. It's a terrific image.
   The image is of this man. (—)
   The man is perceptive.
   The man is caged in his own weak character.

   It's a terrific image—this perceptive man caged in his own weak character.

   John Updike

100

D. The sincere Christian examines each occurrence for the fingerprints of the Providential hand. **(AS)**

George read into each irregular incident possible financial
loss.

The incident could be a greeting in the subway. **(—)**

The incident could be an unscheduled knock on the door.
(. . . —)

As the sincere Christian examines each occurence for the
fingerprints of the Providential hand, George read into
each irregular incident—a greeting in the subway, an
unscheduled knock on the door—possible financial loss.

John Updike

As in previous combining procedures, the underlining indicates what portion of the base sentences should be retained. Notice that when two dashes are
used, one precedes the inserted information and the other follows it.

Problems

Combine each of the following sets of sentences according to the instructions
given. Remember that the **(WHICH/THAT)** instruction may also mean **(JOIN)**.
All the base sentences in this group of problems have been created by breaking down sentences from the works of modern writers.

1. And we have SOMETHING.

They sorely need something. **(WHAT)**

They need a new sense of life's possibilities. **(:)**

James Baldwin

_____

_____

_____

2. I was nine years old.
   Still another woman came. **(WHEN)**
   The woman was <u>Aunt Bessie.</u>
   Aunt Bessie had <u>been living with the Indians.</u> **(WHO)**

   Dorothy M. Johnson

   _____

   _____

   _____

3. This declaration of innocence enraged Bleeker.
   The declaration of innocence was <u>this willingness to take</u>
   <u>blame for acts.</u> **(— . . . —)**
   He hadn't committed <u>the acts.</u> **(WHICH)**

   Frank Rooney

   _____

   _____

   _____

4. She was not at all SOMETHING.
   He had hoped she might be something. **(WHAT)**
   He had hoped she might be <u>sympathetic and helpful.</u> **(—)**

   Conrad Aiken

   _____

   _____

   _____

5. In town he drank several glasses of beer.
   He stood about in Ben Head's saloon. **(AND)**
   The saloon was crowded on Saturday evenings with visiting
   farm hands. **(−)**

Sherwood Anderson

_____

_____

_____

6. Different as they were.
   They were different in background. **(−)**
   They were different in personality.
   They were different in underlying aspiration.
   These two great soldiers had much in common. **(−)**

Bruce Catton

_____

_____

_____

7. There is, after all, another side to the human spirit, too.
   Another side is a dark side. **(− ... −)**

Eric Sevaried

_____

_____

_____

8. The crimes have changed in rapid succession.
   The Jews have been charged with the crimes in the course
      of history. **(WHICH)**
   They were <u>crimes</u>. **(−)**
   The crimes were to justify the atrocities. **(WHICH)**
   The atrocities were <u>perpetrated against them</u>. **(. . . −)**

                                                    Albert Einstein

_____

_____

_____

_____

_____

9. But some obscure and almost unanalyzable drive propelled
      them outward.
   They grew and grew. **(:)**
   They learned and adapted.
   They became the conquerors and defenders of the civilized
      world. **(UNTIL)**

                                                    Gilbert Highet

_____

_____

_____

_____

_____

10. He moves in. **(WHEN)**

Nearly everything else suffers from his intrusion.

It is <u>sometimes because he wants the space and the food</u>. **(—)**

They occupy the space. **(JOIN)**

They eat the food. **(JOIN)**

<u>But</u> it is <u>often simply because his first impulse is "kill it."</u>

He sees a creature or a man. **(WHEN)**

The creature is <u>not of his kind</u>.

The man is <u>not of his race</u>.

Joseph Wood Krutch

_____

_____

_____

_____

_____

11. Open and peaceful competition is something else again.

The competition is <u>for prestige</u>. **(—)**

The competition is <u>for markets</u>.

The competition is <u>for scientific achievement</u>.

The competition is <u>even for men's minds</u>. **(. . . —)**

John F. Kennedy

_____

_____

_____

12. The fantasy is partly physical.
    The interiors are always a little too good. (—)
    The doors are transparent.
    The doors do not really separate one area from another. (ING)
    The carpets are too soft and deep.
    The words are too hard and shallow.
    The corridors are lonely.
    The chairs and facilities are luxurious far beyond the facts of
       international harmony.

    E. B. White

    _____

    _____

    _____

    _____

    _____

    _____

13. The Santa Lucias stood up against the sky to the west.
    They kept the valley from the open sea. (AND)
    They were dark and brooding. (, AND)
    They were unfriendly and dangerous. (—)

    John Steinbeck

    _____

    _____

    _____

    _____

14. Never shall I forget the deep singing of the men at the drum.

The singing of the men at the drum was <u>swelling and sinking</u>.

It was <u>the deepest sound I have heard in all my life</u>.

It was <u>deeper than thunder</u>.

It was <u>deeper than the sound of the Pacific Ocean</u>.

It was <u>deeper than the roar of a deep waterfall</u>.

It was <u>the wonderful deep sound of man</u>. **(:)**

Man was <u>calling to the unspeakable depths</u>.

D. H. Lawrence

_____

_____

_____

_____

_____

_____

15. I had never seen a man beaten.

He had been beaten. **(AS)**

He was <u>this mountain of a man</u>. **(—)**

He <u>died in the battle</u>. **(WHO)**

He had been fighting the battle forty-six years. **(JOIN)**

Jesse Stuart

_____

_____

_____

16. The sky was a clear pale blue.
    It was <u>all in one piece</u>.
    It was in one piece <u>except for the hole</u>. (−)
    The sun made the hole. (**JOIN**)
    <u>And</u> it was <u>fringed around the bottom with treetops</u>. (−)

    Flannery O'Connor

_____

_____

_____

_____

24. Challenge

The combinations you will write in this section make use of combining signals you have learned.

Problems

Combine each of the following sets of sentences according to the instructions given. If, after you have written the combined version of a set of sentences, you think the idea might be better expressed in a somewhat different way, revise the sentence as you see fit. For example, since many of the sentences are quite long, you might want to express the same idea in two or three shorter sentences. You might want to combine the base sentences in a different order, ignoring the signals supplied.

1. Police officials returned from a tour.
   The police officials were <u>American</u>.
   The tour was <u>of Japan</u>.
   They were <u>impressed by Tokyo</u>.
   The crime rate is low in Tokyo despite SOMETHING. **(WHERE)**
   Eleven-and-a-half million people live there. **(THE FACT THAT)**

_____

_____

_____

_____

_____

_____

2. Ramon was chatting with Miss Slater.
Miss Slater was the redhead from Utah.
The redhead from Utah had started eating fish and chips. **(WHO)**
She discovered SOMETHING. **(AS SOON AS)**
Nicholas was really an Englishman and not a traveling actor. **(THAT)**
The actor was after her money.

_____

_____

_____

_____

3. Two physicians recently claimed SOMETHING.
The physicians were West German.
Massive doses of enzymes and vitamin A have destroyed tumors. **(THAT)**
The tumors were malignant.
These doses prevented SOMETHING. **(AND)**
The cells spread. **(THE SPREAD + OF)**
The cells were cancerous.
This made SOMETHING possible. **(ING)**
Patients live lives. **(IT . . . FOR . . . TO)**
Patients suffer from cancer. **(ING)**
The lives are near-normal.

_____

_____

_____

_____

4. SOMETHING convinced the interrogators (of) SOMETHING.
   Their captive couldn't explain SOMETHING. **(THE FACT THAT)**
   Their captive was <u>English-speaking</u>.
   Their captive claimed to be an American soldier. **(WHO)**
   "Sunny side up" meant something. **(WHAT)**
   Babe Ruth was someone. **(AND WHO)**
   He was an enemy spy. **(THAT)**

   _____

   _____

   _____

   _____

5. SOMETHING doesn't matter.
   We've traveled so far. **(IT . . . HOW FAR)**
   What really matters is SOMETHING. **(;)**
   We have yet to go so far. **(HOW FAR)**

   _____

   _____

6. Dorothy left the area. **(AFTER)**
   Things began to happen.
   The things were strange things. **(—)**
   She had predicted the things. **(THAT)**

   _____

   _____

   _____

7. Her students were greatly relieved.
   Professor Jollimore clarified her ideas.
   Professor Jollimore was a scholar.
   The scholar was brilliant.
   The scholar was renowned.
   Her ideas had been difficult to understand.
   They had been explained in purely mathematical terms in
     her book.

   _____

   _____

   _____

   _____

8. He was running gracefully.
   He was running effortlessly.
   His legs were skimming over the track.
   Young Carlson wondered SOMETHING.
   Young Carlson had been training for six long years.
   He could run the mile so fast that morning.
   The morning was quiet.
   The morning was cool.

   _____

   _____

   _____

   _____

9. It was immediately after the Depression.
   Work was scarce. **(WHEN)**
   He married.
   He quit teaching shop at the local high school.
   He started SOMETHING. **(AND)**
   He made small machine parts. **(ING)**
   First he made them for a few local businesses. **(—)**
   Then he made them for several small manufacturers. **(AND)**
   Finally he began SOMETHING. **(UNTIL)**
   He supplied the industrial giants of New England and the
   Great Lakes. **(ING)**

   _____

   _____

   _____

   _____

   _____

10. We arrived.
    The starter fired his gun.
    We were late again.
    We struggled to find seats.
    We tried to watch the race at the same time.

    _____

    _____

    _____

    _____

11. The family was not convinced.
    Jerry tried to explain away SOMETHING as a case of sleep-
        walking. (WHEN)
    He was discovered in the kitchen. ('S + ING)
    He was discovered at midnight.
    He was eating a sundae.
    The sundae was hot fudge.
    The sundae was smothered with cream.
    The cream was whipped.
    The sleepwalking was brought on by nervous tension.

    _____

    _____

    _____

    _____

12. You are alone with your thoughts.
    You can see things more clearly.
    You can sort out SOMETHING.
    Something has happened.
    You can make plans.
    You can focus all your attention on yourself.
    You are someone.
    You are heading somewhere.

    _____

    _____

    _____

    _____

13. SOMETHING doesn't matter.
    You say something. (IT . . . WHAT)
    We still don't know SOMETHING. (:)
    We are to prevent SOMETHING somehow. (HOW TO)
    That developer destroys the coastal wetlands thoughtlessly.
    ('S + ~~LY~~ + DESTRUCTION + OF)

    _____

    _____

    _____

    _____

14. He stood there.
    His face was twitching in pain. (WITH)
    To be in pain at all was bad enough. (—)
    SOMETHING was almost beyond his bearing. (;)
    His friends abandoned him. (FOR . . . TO)

    _____

    _____

    _____

    _____

15. SOMETHING surprises me.
    No one has asked SOMETHING. (IT . . . THAT)
    Ray's solar heater works somehow. (HOW)
    It cost so much to build. (AND + HOW MUCH)

    _____

    _____

16. He sat back in his chair.
   He dreamed. **(AND)**
   He dreamed of sunlight.
   He dreamed of air.
   The air was sweet.
   The air was clear.
   He dreamed of water. **(AND)**
   The water was sparkling.
   But it was only a dream. **(,)**
   Those things were long gone from the earth. **(:)**
   SOMETHING was foolish. **(AND)**
   A cave-dweller imagined SOMETHING. **(IT . . . FOR . . . TO)**
   Times were like something before SOMETHING. **(WHAT)**
   The Final War came. **(THE COMING + OF)**

_____

_____

_____

_____

_____

_____

_____

_____

_____

17. He claimed SOMETHING. **(ING)**

    Transcendental Meditation is a proven method of SOMETHING.
       (THAT)

    It eliminates drug abuse. **(ING)**

    It curbs criminal tendencies. **(ING)**

    It improves physical health. **(AND + ING)**

    Jeff Parmet explained SOMETHING.

    Jeff Parmet is an instructor in the technique.

    A student learns SOMETHING. **(THAT)**

    One is to go into a trance somehow. **(HOW TO)**

    He spends 20 minutes twice a day. **(ING)**

    He lets his mind dwell on a "mantra." **(ING)**

    A "mantra" is a sound.

    The sound is meaningless.

    The "mantra" is selected for him by his teacher.

    _____

    _____

    _____

    _____

    _____

    _____

    _____

    _____

    _____

Writing Workshop

1. The Platypus

Consider the following material the rough notes for a piece of writing on one of nature's oddities—the duck-billed platypus. Select what you consider the most interesting and informative details, put them into sentence form, organize them into a few paragraphs, and write a description of the platypus using as many sentence-combining techniques as you can. Your writing need not necessarily be in the usual essay or report form—you might base a story or poem on the platypus.

As an alternative, choose another of nature's oddities and write on it.

Platypus

warm blooded
furry
lactates like a mammal
lays eggs like a lizard
dredges food from stream bottoms
    with its bill
bill is duck-like
lives in a burrow
bill-slate gray
2 small closely-spaced nostrils
    for air and smelling
eyes set high in head for scanning
    and lookout

reptilelike ears
amber-colored fur
    coarse on outside
    soft next to skin
large flat tail—used as a rudder
stubby sprawling legs
5-toed paws
    heavy webs for swimming
    heavy claws for digging
blindly nuzzles stream bottom
    with sensitive bill
bill soft—not like duck

118

eats prawns, worms, insect larvae
    crushable mollusks
eats tadpoles, grubs, beetles
chews at surface of water
1200 worms and 50 crayfish a day (!)

keen hearing/fair eyesight
slight growl
doesn't shiver
doesn't sweat

young a half inch long

eggs have leathery membrane
    like lizard
legs stubby like reptile
no teeth—hornlike plate
    (tooth at birth to break egg)
bill a mass of nerves
nerves relay tactile sensations

nest—leaves
lives in tunnel
lays 2 eggs
eggs cemented by sticky casings

During nursing, mother eats as much as her body weight in food every day

Teaches swimming/hunting   Lives in Australia

2. Designing for the Future

One of human beings' unique talents is their ability to imagine the nonexistent and create the extraordinary. Can you imagine, for example, the house or city of the future; forms of transportation in the twenty-first century; or a computer-programmed psychological aide that would solve problems, eliminate danger, and keep a person in a constantly "happy" state?

Design some system, gadget, machine, building or other creation that might enrich future life. What does it look like? What does it do? How does it function? Make a list of your "thing's" characteristics in rough note form. Then organize your material into a several-paragraph description. Add a drawing or schematic diagram if you wish.

25. The Professionals

In this section you will be combining base sentences into sentences that were originally written by professional writers—people who have made their living manipulating language. The styles of these writers are quite varied, and yet the sentences of each can be "reconstituted" using sentence-combining techniques.

Problems

Write out each set of bases as one sentence according to the instructions given. After you've written the combinations you may wish to experiment with alternative ways of expressing the same information.

1. SOMETHING seems likely.
    The Appalachians will continue going down. (IT . . . THAT)
    Its lovely mountains and hills will house a culture. (, THAT)
    The culture will be of poverty and despair.
    It will become a reservation. (AND THAT)
    The reservation will be for the old.
    The reservation will be for the apathetic.
    The reservation will be for the misfits. (AND)

                                                  Michael Harrington

_____

_____

_____

_____

_____

2. The Kid was yanked to his feet by Harry Street.
   He was <u>slapped on the back by Karl Case.</u>
   He was <u>surrounded by the entire team.</u>
   The entire team emerged from the dugout. **(WHO)**
   They were <u>dancing</u> with delight.
   They were <u>cheering with delight.</u> **(AND)**

   John R. Tunis

   _____

   _____

   _____

   _____

   _____

3. It was just SOMETHING.
   I had never seen SOMETHING as being possible. **(THAT)**
   He pulled a chick on the outside. **(IT . . . FOR . . . TO)**
   She was a <u>nice-looking chick like this Ruth.</u>

   Claude Brown

   _____

   _____

   _____

   _____

   _____

4. It was some time.

All the sirens in the suburb took up my glad tidings. **(BEFORE)**

The sirens took them up like a choir of archangels.

The archangels were iron-lunged.

The archangels were overenthusiastic.

All the sirens made the night rise and fall.

All the sirens made dreams flare up and crash.

All the sirens crept into the ears of the population.

The population was sleeping.

All the sirens transformed the moon into a light. **(AND)**

The moon was cold.

The moon was disinterested.

The light was merciless.

There was no way to block out the light. **(THAT)**

Günter Grass

_____

_____

_____

_____

_____

_____

_____

_____

5. I'm going to remember everything.
   I'm going to remember the jails. (**—**)
   I been in the jails. (**JOIN**)
   I'm going to remember the cops. (**AND**)
   The cops beat me. (**THAT**)
   I'm going to remember SOMETHING. (**AND**)
   I spent so long a time screaming and stinking. (**HOW LONG**)
   I was screaming and stinking in my own dirt.
   I tried to break my habit. (**ING**)

   James Baldwin

---

6. The tavern was barnlike.
   It had a bar. (**WITH**)
   The bar was short.
   The bar was blunt.
   A few men dawdled. (**AT WHICH**)
   The men had inexpressive faces. (**WITH**)

   Bernard Malamud

124

7. I got the audience's attention. **(ONCE)**
   I could start talking.
   I could tell them about my home in St. Louis. **(,)**
   The home was so cold the snow wouldn't melt on the floor.
   I could tell them about the bed.
   The bed was so crowded we had to leave bookmarks to save
     our place.
   We got up to go to the toilet. **(WHEN)**
   We went to the toilet in the middle of the night.

Dick Gregory

_____

_____

_____

_____

_____

_____

8. The girl's face was there.
   It was really quite beautiful in memory.
   It was astonishing, in fact. **(:)**

Ray Bradbury

_____

_____

_____

9. Montag did not look back at his wife.
   He went along the hall to the kitchen. **(AS)**
   He went <u>trembling</u>.
   He stood a long time. **(WHERE)**
   He watched the rain. **(ING)**
   The rain <u>hit the windows</u>.
   He came back down the hall in the light. **(BEFORE)**
   The light was <u>gray</u>.
   He waited for the tremble to subside. **(ING)**

Ray Bradbury

_____

_____

_____

_____

10. I pulled off my shirt and pants.
    I <u>got into work clothes</u>
    I <u>went back to the other room to tell them</u> SOMETHING. **(AND)**
    I had decided to go to jail. **(JOIN)**

Martin Luther King, Jr.

_____

_____

_____

_____

11. I walked into my office.
    I opened the door wide. **(AND)**
    Anybody could see me there. **(SO THAT)**
    Anybody wanted to look. **(WHO)**
    I shuffled papers and layouts. **(ING)**

                                                James Dickey

_____

_____

_____

_____

_____

12. A white woman stood directly in front of them.
    The white woman was poised on the edge of the
       embankment.
    The embankment was opposite.
    Her hat was in her hand.
    Her hair was lit by the sun.

                                                Richard Wright

_____

_____

_____

_____

13. The two soldier-sons were home on leave.
The <u>younger one</u> was <u>with his new girl-friend</u>.
She was <u>a</u> girl.
The girl was <u>tall</u>.
The girl was <u>gay</u>.
The girl was <u>pretty</u>.
The girl was <u>named Margie</u>.
She had <u>dark hair</u>. **(WITH)**
She had <u>brown eyes</u>.
She had <u>a lovely little golden mole on her cheek</u>. **(AND)**
The girl <u>helped Mother in the kitchen</u>. **(WHO)**
The girl <u>sipped sherry</u>.
The girl <u>sang snatches of songs</u>. **(AND)**
She <u>tossed back her hair</u>. **(ING)**
Her hair was <u>long</u>.
Her hair was <u>loose</u>.

Christy Brown

_____

_____

_____

_____

_____

_____

_____

_____

14. Harry Brubaker was alone in a spot in a war.
    He was <u>a twenty-nine year-old lawyer from Denver, Colorado.</u>
    He had never intended to defend the spot. **(JOIN)**
    He had not understood the war. **(JOIN)**

James A. Michener

_____

_____

_____

_____

_____

15. He hurried to the kitchen door.
    He <u>hung outside there some minutes.</u> **(BUT)**
    He entered. **(BEFORE)**
    He <u>stood for some minutes more inside.</u> **(AND)**
    He closed it after him. **(BEFORE)**

Zora Neale Hurston

_____

_____

_____

_____

16. Riley was silent.
    Riley looked down to the end of the porch. **(ING)**
    At the end of the porch the sun had eaten a square into the
       shade. **(WHERE)**
    The sun fixed a butterfly in its brilliance. **(ING)**
    The butterfly was flitting.
    The square was bright.

                                           Ralph W. Ellison

    _____

    _____

    _____

    _____

    _____

17. He explained to me with great insistence SOMETHING.
    Every question possessed a power. **(THAT)**
    The power did not lie in the answer. **(THAT)**

                                           Elie Wiesel

    _____

    _____

    _____

    _____

18. I can die. **(AND IF)**
    I have brought any light. **(ING)**
    I have exposed any truth. **(ING)**
    The truth is meaningful.
    The truth will help to destroy the cancer. **(THAT)**
    The cancer is racist.
    The cancer is malignant in the body of America. **(THAT)**
    Then, all of the credit is due to Allah. **(—)**

                    Malcolm X

_____

_____

_____

_____

19. We start them sooner and sooner in school.
    We make a farce of graduations. **(AND)**
    The graduations are even from kindergarten now. **(—)**
    School becomes a rat race. **(. . . — + UNTIL)**
    The rat race never has a home stretch in sight. **(WITH)**

                  Bruno Bettelheim

_____

_____

_____

_____

20. Bond's eyes narrowed to slits.
    He scanned them. **(AS)**
    He was <u>measuring</u>.
    He was <u>estimating</u>.

    Ian Fleming

---

21. SOMETHING was a pleasure.
    He walked up and down the long corridors. **(IT ... FOR ... TO)**
    He flipped hellos to the friends. **(ING)**
    The friends were <u>new</u>.
    He was making friends. **(JOIN)**

    Gordon Parks

22. They leaped up and down.
    They were <u>screaming</u>.
    They were <u>clapping their hands</u>. **(AND)**
    Their hats were <u>falling back on their shoulders</u>.
    Their <u>hair</u> was <u>flying wild</u>.

    Katherine Anne Porter

26. On Your Own

No combining signals have been given for any of the sets of sentences in this section. All the combining decisions are yours to make — not only how to combine a set of sentences, but also how many combined sentences to make from the set.

1. Tonio was listening to Miss Harper.
   Miss Harper was a former beauty queen.
   She is now an entomologist of some note.
   He wondered SOMETHING.
   Human beings consider physical appearance so important for some reason.
   They find insects repulsive.
   The insects are the most fascinating.
   They find cars beautiful.
   The cars are the gaudiest.
   They honor a woman for her face and figure.
   They ignore SOMETHING.
   She has something to say.

   _____

   _____

   _____

   _____

   _____

   _____

   _____

2. SOMETHING made Andrew decide SOMETHING.
   He learned SOMETHING.
   Vanessa hadn't arrived yet.
   The plans must be changed.
   Without her report they wouldn't know SOMETHING.
   Her report was on wind patterns.
   The wind patterns were in the mountain passes.
   The mountain passes were snow-choked.
   They were to drop the supplies somewhere.
   The supplies were for climbers.
   The climbers were stranded.
   He had no choice.
   He'd have to fly in alone.
   He'd know the danger.
   He'd guess at the route.
   He'd hope to make it through.

_____

_____

_____

_____

_____

_____

_____

_____

3. We live in a valley.
   Floods are common here.
   SOMETHING is laughable.
   A group of investors plans a housing development.
   The investors are eager.
   The investors are from out of state.
   The development is to replace the cranberry bogs.
   The bogs are in the lowlands.
   The lowlands are along the river.
   They tell us SOMETHING.
   SOMETHING is old-fashioned.
   We point out SOMETHING.
   Their scheme is foolish.

_____

_____

_____

_____

_____

_____

_____

_____

_____

_____

4. A search revealed SOMETHING.
   The search was conducted by the fire marshall's office.
   Old rags had been stored near SOMETHING.
   The rags were still damp with solvents.
   The solvents were flammable.
   The solvents were for cleaning.
   Something seemed to be a heater.
   The heater was small and portable.
   The heater was fired by kerosene.
   Beside a heater is a dangerous spot for anything flammable.

   _____

   _____

   _____

   _____

   _____

   _____

   _____

   _____

   _____

   _____

   _____

   _____

5. We waited for hours.
   All of us were told SOMETHING.
   All of us were in the lobby.
   The lobby was stifling.
   Dr. Wainright's announcement had been premature.
   The satellite photos had not indicated SOMETHING.
   There is intelligent life on Jupiter.
   He mistook SOMETHING for the city.
   A shadow was cast by the satellite itself.
   The city was large.
   The city was floating.
   The city was described in his press release.

   _____

   _____

   _____

   _____

   _____

   _____

MNOPQRS—08543
PRINTED IN THE UNITED STATES OF AMERICA